T0113867

Most of our daily conversations are focused on the issue of flesh. Just as Jesus pointed out, it is mostly related to what to eat, drink, and wear. However, suppose our conversations began with the flesh and ended with the flesh. In that case, we miss the opportunity to convey God's message and save the spirit.

-from this book-

Jesus's Dialogue

for our daily talking

JOHN H.S. LEE

WESTBOW
PRESS®
A DIVISION OF THOMAS NELSON
& ZONDERVAN

WestBow Press books may be ordered through booksellers or by contacting:

WestBow Press
A Division of Thomas Nelson & Zondervan
1663 Liberty Drive
Bloomington, IN 47403
www.westbowpress.com
844-714-3454

Scripture quotations are taken from The Holy Bible, New International Version®, NIV® Copyright © 1973, 1978, 1984, 2011 by Biblica, Inc.® Used by permission. All rights reserved worldwide.

ISBN: 978-1-6642-8548-4 (sc)
ISBN: 978-1-6642-8550-7 (hc)
ISBN: 978-1-6642-8549-1 (e)

Library of Congress Control Number: 2022922507

Print information available on the last page.

WestBow Press rev. date: 12/23/2022

Contents

Preface

Just as Jesus showed God, our Christian lives should be able to reveal God to our neighbors. This book attempts to find the answer through Jesus's conversations about how we can show God in our daily encounters and conversations.

The questions are how to defend Christianity and how to evangelize. These remain challenging daily tasks for many Christians. There is no methodological approach to how to do it in this area. It's not because of a lack of biblical knowledge or learning. Instead, we don't have a model for such conversations. Nor do we have the specific communication skills or methods of evangelism; that is, when, how, and what to say.

The discovery of Jesus's dialogue breaks down the barriers between faith and reality. It quenches our long-standing thirst and questions our daily encounters and conversations at once.

When the missionary Bu-seon Han (Bruce F. Hunt, 1903–1992) was alive, I got a commentary[1] from his small private library at Kosin University in Yeongdo, Korea. It was a time when it was difficult to obtain original texts, so I bought several Bible-related books out of my hunger for books. That commentary is one of them. I thought I would read it in the future.

Forty years passed, and I came across this book again, after spending much time stained with ignorance and making many

---

[1] William Hendriksen, *Gospel of John* (1959). The banner of truth trust, London.

mistakes in my Christian life. After reading the commentary, I became deeply interested in Jesus's conversation.

Reading this, I met Jesus Christ and was deeply fascinated by the way Jesus communicated. I was amazed at the diversity, delicacy, and kindness that Jesus shown, which I had overlooked before. The content of the conversation and the skill came to me as valuable things, especially in his approaching and leading people. I still can't forget the joy of finding it.

The gospel of John contains a relatively large number of detailed conversations with Jesus. The talks, occurring in various situations, teach us what to say and to convey evangel as a golden rule. I tried to sort it out on my own.

Jesus's conversation tells us what attitude we should take and how we speak. It also introduces an aggressive conversational form that leads to dialogues. In particular, it is gratifying to discover that there is a specific frame in Jesus's dialogue evangelism method. This book introduces it and shows how to use field materials as effective means of conveying the truth in daily life. It also introduces the way, how to cope with the frictions and assaults that Jesus had shown.

Jesus's conversation will guide us on the following points. First, it shows a conversational model and introduces us to dealing with conversations in confidence. It shows that exchanges should have active means of defensive and offensive methods in evangelism.

Second, it enables us to turn our daily encounters into valuable ministry sites. Most of our lives stand in the field of unbelief. It is a blind spot where the Word of God does not reach directly. However, we cannot ignore that because it is the field of our living, and that is the foundation of the Christian life. The conversation of Jesus can be used as a practice ground to save lives even in the field of unbelief. It teaches us to find out what can change in them and how to convey the Word of God.

Third, it nurtures and maintains my spirituality. I have found that Jesus's conversation is the most realistic and closest way to defend my faith. It indicates how our dialogue in today's life should go. And at the same time, it is a way for us to defend our beliefs and actively deliver the message of God. That is what it means to live everyday lives in the presence of the Holy Spirit.

Jesus demonstrated this way of life. He accomplished the work he wanted to do through encounters and conversations. He could conclude that he always did good work for Father: "The one who sent me is with me; he has not left me alone, for I always do what pleases him" (John 8:29).Isn't this what Jesus is talking about, the lifestyle of always and doing the things that are pleasing to him that Jesus taught through his ministry and numerous encounters?

The phrase, "He has not left me alone," also tells us that God's presence always follows the work of doing what pleases him. The work pleasing to God is to accomplish his will, which lies in knowing him and believing in the Son, Jesus Christ.

Also, "together" means to dwell in one relationship with God.

It is not difficult to see that this confession is for the disciples' teachings, not for his own. Thus, it will not be strange to say that faith stands on the ground of daily encounters and conversations. The answer to ministry is to focus it on our daily lives.

Many try to find ways to keep their beliefs, but few find them. Hopefully, the study of Jesus's dialogue will boost our beliefs and guide us to find our necessary tasks. The awareness of the importance of daily encounters will make us constantly devote ourselves to better conversations.

I want to share this article with those who ask, "How can I defend my faith?" and, "What should I say?"[2]

---

[2] Interpretation of this text was mainly based on and referenced William Hendriksen, *Gospel of John*, "Commentary" (1959) The banner of truth trust, London.

Chapter 1

JESUS'S DIALOGUE

JESUS'S CONVERSATION CAN BE EXPRESSED IN VARIOUS WAYS depending on one's point of view. That would mean it's so big. It is not easy to define Jesus's conversation in one or two words, but if we summarize it from how we should communicate, we can say it has two characteristics.

1. LEADING DIALOGUE

The education of disciples that flows throughout the Gospels reveals Jesus as an eternal teacher. Jesus led disciples with patience to reach confession on their own through trials and errors. In the eyes of the disciples, Jesus first appeared as a mighty national Savior, like Moses. Gradually, their eyes opened from teachers to masters, to Messiah, to son of God, and to God. Keeping pace with the spiritual growth of the early disciples of Jesus Christ, the eternal teacher, gradually led to a confession in their hearts. Sometimes confession was reached at once, and sometimes little by little. As we shared more experiences, confession became more solid.

As faith and confession cannot simply be given or forced

but arise from inside, it is valuable. Jesus didn't hurry to reveal his identity and try to gain disciples to have enlightenment individually. It took three and a half years of trial and error through personal encounters and conversations. Finally, they found the love of Father through the cross and were able to confess Jesus Christ as Lord fully.

The same goes for conversations. Jesus applied the truth itself, and the transmission of that truth depended on the person's faith. By knowing the person and conveying the Word of God in a way that corresponded to it, Jesus led the listeners to come to confession on their own.

The relatively lengthy dialogues in the gospel of John have a specific frame. I call this type of dialogue "Jesus's four-step dialogue evangelism." Although straightforward, it contains all the elements necessary for evangelism, such as curiosity, supplementary explanation, rebuke, and application and invitation. It leads the conversation itself. It allows us to approach naturally in real situations, and it is an effective conversational technique. What's more, isn't that the method the Lord himself used?

First, Jesus's conversational style can be presented naturally in our daily encounters and conversations, leading and making conversation to easily convey the gospel.

Suppose the self-centered dialogue focuses on understanding and persuading others. In that case, Jesus's unique method of evangelism shows God and elevates one's faith to confession. In this respect, it is different from the evangelism method we usually use. The dialogue proceeds through supplementary explanations according to the listeners' reactions rather than one-sided preaching or persuasion.

This pattern appears in long conversations such as with Nicodemus, the Samaritan woman, the conversation with the Jews the day after the great miracle of the five loaves and two fishes, and the conversations with Martha, also an opponent of Jewish religious leaders.

Jesus's conversational style unwittingly draws in other people. Nicodemus's dialogue also draws attention to this aspect, probably because it was presented naturally to him without him even knowing it. The dialogue includes a person's path to salvation from born-again and the Holy Spirit, the Son of Man and God's love, the resolution of sins and judgment, and the invitation to eternal life. Also, in a conversation with a Samaritan woman, Jesus gradually opens the woman's perspective. Her eyes are opened from the Jew to the prophet and finally to the Messiah. His leading dialogue is outstanding.

Jesus's conversation was about showing God to each person. It stated that humans could only be changed when they met God. There can be no more real driving force for change than this. It leads to fundamental, entire, and intensive change. The way Jesus led from the first meeting with the six disciples clearly shows this.

The first meeting with the disciples at the beginning of the ministry was impressive. The encounters and conversations of the young people—Andrew, John, Peter, James, Philip, and Nathanael—can be summarized as meeting God individually and coming to immediate, individual confessions.

Andrew and John came to Jesus through the introduction of their teacher, John the Baptist. Disciple John remembered precisely when he first met Jesus, around ten o'clock. Considering that the scripture was written in his old age, sixty years later, it is easy to guess how precious and impressive his first meeting with Jesus was personally; it changed his entire life. He might not forget his first calling: "What do you want?" "Come," and, "You will see"(John 1:38).These are the first words spoken to him when he turned and saw them following. He asked, "What do you want?" not, "Who do you want?"He said he already knew their needs and called them with the answer. The two stayed together that evening at the invitation of Jesus. The next day, Andrew's first step was to find his brother Simon and tell him, "We have found the Messiah" (John1:41).They saw the Messiah. How could one come to such a great confession overnight? It is surprising. There is no record of any miracle performed that evening. It will be revealed through conversations.

Although the details of conversations of that day are not recorded, we can assume that the Messiah was confirmed by unraveling what Moses and several prophets recorded, as shown in Philip's expression. Same as with the conversation with the two disciples on their way to Emmaus after the resurrection.

As Peter approached, he paid attention to him and gave him a new name, Cephas ("Rock"). It does not simply foretell the future but promises God's grace to help Peter to achieve throughout his life.

Nathanael, who approached through Philip's introduction, must have been surprised when he heard the praise, "Here truly is an Israelite, in whom there is no deceit"(John 1:47).In his question, a big surprise is expressed through rhetorical negation of "How do you know me?"(John1:48).Unexpectedly, he came to Jesus with skepticism over the urging of his friend Philip. He said, "Nazareth! Can anything good come from there?"(John1:46).In other words, what can be expected in the countryside of Galilee? But when Jesus told Nathanael that he had seen him praying under the fig tree before Philip called him, he should have been astonished and must have felt Jesus's divinity. His immediate confession followed:"Rabbi, you are the Son of God; you are the King of Israel"(John 1:49).

If we deepen our understanding of Jesus, we can easily discover how deeply his insights and understanding of life are. He geared up faith with his omnipotence and omniscience by showing God directly or expanding one's perspective. The disciples confessed the omniscience of Jesus when the end drew near:"Now we can see that you know all things and that you do not even need to have anyone ask you questions. This makes us believe that you came from God" (John 16:30).

It is also found that the fourth gospel writer implicitly

emphasizes the omniscience of Jesus in knowing and dealing with life at the beginning of the passage, the end of John 2. The expression is, "He did not need any testimony about mankind, for he knew what was in each person"(John2: 24–25). Besides the story's contents, we can guess his intentions were to stress that he knew people and led conversations. Starting with the conversation between Nicodemus, a Jewish ruler, and a woman from Sychar in Samaria, he allocated a lot of space to the entire conversation in detail.

The next day, Jesus met Philip, a villager, who was with Andrew and Peter from Bethesda. Philip's confession is also well expressed to his friend Nathanael. "We have found the one Moses wrote about in the Law, and about whom the prophets also wrote—Jesus of Nazareth, the son of Joseph" (John 1:45).

Furthermore, Jesus proclaimed an incredible, unimaginable vision to the six young men with Nathanael in that field. "You believe because I told you I saw you under the fig tree. You will see greater things than that" (John1:50). He added, "Very truly I tell you, you shall see heaven open, and the angels of God ascending and descending on the Son of Man" (John1:51).That is the vision of a spiritual Messiah, who will open the heavens and accomplish God's work beyond the Messiah as the national leader they expect. This vision was realized a long time later by the disciples. All of this happened within just two days. It's amazing.[3]

In addition, Jesus's conversations were meant to approach each person's soul and build up that individual's faith through personal caring and amazingly detailed consideration. This model shows how we could approach our neighbors.

It can be seen the same way when he asked a sick man lying by the pool of Bethesda, "Do you want to get well?" (John 5:6). This patient must have been hoping for recovery for a longtime. Even with the obvious answer, he asked whether he was trying to

---

[3] William Hendriksen, *Gospel of John* (1959), Refer topp.102–107.

prepare the patient's mind rather than simply trying to cure the disease. It was thoughtful to open the patient's awareness to the fact he had no chance of getting better on his own. This patient had been suffering from the disease for thirty-eight years. The patient's words show that his soul was in deep frustration and in a pathological state. Such is the expression of resentment: "Sir, I have no one to help me into the pool when the water is stirred. While I am trying to get in, someone else goes down ahead of me" (John5:7).

It was a matter of survival and spoke well of the fierce and heartless reality. When these words were spoken, we can imagine that an unexpected new vitality arose in this patient. When this long-forgotten seeker saw this stranger's eyes, which seemed to consider his deepest pains and needs with compassion, he realized that was the only chance to appeal to him, and that is reflected in his sayings. Behind this patient's answer, he held onto the strong hope that this stranger might give him a chance to go to the pond first, or there might be some other possibility of recovery. Jesus gave this word on the premise that he had the will to heal him. The reality was that it was impossible to find another opportunity; this could be his last hope. He heard a tremendous command in a single expectation: "Get up! Pick up your mat and walk" (John 5:8).How challenging and authoritative that was! With his prepared heart, he accepted these words. He must have felt the power of the Word healed him at once. The long paralysis that robbed him of thirty-eight years was completely healed at once, and he enjoyed the joy of a new life (John 5:1–18).[4]

The same was true of what happened the night after the great miracle of the five loaves and two fishes. It is believed to be between three and six in the morning. The boat was against the wind and suffered from the bashing waves. At least a twelve-man rowing

---

[4] William Hendriksen, *Gospel of John* (1959) Refer to chapter 5, pp. 191–197.

boat rarely moved forward in the face of such a headwind. Being in the middle of the sea on a windy, wavy night was terrifying. Without the experience of facing such a situation, the terrifying feeling when a ship drifts in a strong wind is hard to imagine. The disciples were in an isolated situation. What occupied their sight was, in a word, the fear of the ship sinking or floating away. Those fears seized slowly as human efforts were exhausted.

Even the fears of the disciples, well-trained fishermen, were painful. When they reached the middle of the lake, their boat was facing west, so they would have rowed east. These boatmen could discern the outlines of a figure walking on the water. It was approaching quickly despite the strong wind and was gradually overtaking the boat. The fishermen were fearful until the moment came, as if he was about to pass them by. Then the disciples shouted, "It's a ghost" (Matthew 14:26).At night, dark-blue waves crashed against the ship's railings; those with weak hearts fainted when they saw it. The raging waves and strong winds frightened them. And their sight had completely forgotten the green pastures and the power of Jesus to feed the crowd hours earlier.

As Jesus was heading toward the boat, he deliberately tried to go as if passing the boat. Why did he do this? It was not to scare them away. It was a considerate action to avoid the extreme fear of the disciples. Then he spoke to them: "Take courage! It is I. Don't be afraid" (Matthew 14:27).The fear of death would have immediately turned into a sense of relief and awe.[5]

The caring and detailed description of the two disciples walking to Emmaus and Mary Magdalene can also be seen as leading to confession.

Jesus approached the two disciples like an ordinary passerby. They said that the crucifixion of Jesus was a shocking event, that Jesus was a prophet, and though he had heard of his resurrection,

---

[5] William Hendriksen, *Gospel of John* ((1959) Refer to chapter 6,pp. 224-225.

he had hopes but was not certain (Luke 24:18–24). It was getting dark as they went on their way. Jesus pretended not to know them and approached the disciples. Indeed, he was the subject of the resurrection, he already knew these disciples. He may have had many other ways in which he could manifest himself. "What are you discussing together as you walk along?" (Luke 24:17). "What things?"He asked questions that might reach them and lead them to confess by opening their eyes. It was to open their slow and hesitant hearts. Through rebukes, he brought the light to their darkened and obtuse minds: "How foolish you are, and how slow to believe all that the prophets have spoken! Did not the Messiah have to suffer these things and then enter his glory?" (Luke 24:25–26). While telling the details of the resurrection that had been fulfilled according to scripture, their eyes opened, and their hearts warmed. How considerate is that? Isn't it an amazing approach?

A similar case happened with Mary Magdalene. After being healed, she followed Jesus like a shadow along with Mary, the mother of Jesus, and Salome, his aunt, taking care of him and his disciples. In the crucifixion scene, Mary Magdalene took part in the funeral, watching him until the end. While it was still dark, she went to Jesus's tomb in the early morning of the first day after the Sabbath. When she saw that the body of Jesus was gone, she ran and reported to Peter and John and followed them back to the tomb. After the two disciples left, she wept in front of the tomb. When Jesus appeared, he first asked Mary, "woman, why are you crying? who is it you are looking for?" (John 20:15).It seemed to have nothing to do with this incident. Again, since he was the subject of the resurrection, why did he pretend not to know? Why would he hide the good news of the resurrection from Mary, who loved him the most, who did not recognize him at first.

The disappearance of the body was an unusual and shocking event. Her attention was focused on retrieving the body. Even with the angel's notification, she did not realize that Jesus had been resurrected. When she turned around and saw Jesus she did not realize he was Jesus. She thought he was a gardener and asked him to hand over the body of Jesus. Then Jesus called her by name, "Miriam!"[6] It was the familiar dialect of her hometown to call to her. It was just a single voice, but it must have been soft and warm. It must have been a moment when her eyes suddenly opened, freeing her dark and trapped sight.

This meeting of the resurrected Jesus and Mary Magdalene is perhaps the most moving scene recorded in the synoptic gospels, Matthew, Mark, and Luke. It must have been a moment of silence where inexpressible fear and joy, surprise and intimacy intersect implicitly. As she began to open her eyes to the resurrection, she said, "Rabboni!"(John20:16). ("Rabboni" is the highest honorific title for a rabbi and refers to leaders like Gamaliel.)

When she tried to touch him, Jesus told her, "Do not hold onto me, for I have not yet ascended to the Father" (John 20:17), confirming the resurrected body. He instilled in her the fact about the resurrection, which came to her as reality and faith. Confession is impossible to say without deep inner consideration. No one can confess Jesus as the Lord without realizing that he is Christ. It would be easy to reveal simply who he is. But I think Jesus took the slow way to lead her to the confession of the Messiah. Confession is so precious because it is not given as a transfer or coercion of knowledge.[7]

Jesus's conversations are applied differently when conveying the gospel; they are not in the same form. Jesus treated and spoke to people according to their beliefs. Simply put, his conversations were customized.

Jesus also took different approaches to curing the sick. For example, in Mark chapter 7, the story of the healing of a deaf and

---

[6] William Hendriksen, *Gospel of John* ((1959) Refer to chapter 6, p. 457.

[7] William Hendriksen, *Gospel of John* (1959) Refer to chapter 6, pp. 447–457.

stuttering man is recorded, and the method of healing is a little different from other cases. He put his fingers in the patient's ears, spit, and touched his tongue. And the man was healed.

Why didn't he heal immediately and easily? That part is difficult and can be interpreted several ways. I think it must have been the careful consideration of Jesus in this aspect. In other words, from the standpoint of the sick, Jesus treated him according to his belief. The point is that this sick man was deaf, so he might not have known what people were talking about or why they brought him to Jesus. Placing his hand on his ear rendered his will to heal his ear. Even spitting and putting his hand on his tongue also gave him faith.

Mark chapter 8 records the healing of blind man at Bethsaida. Jesus spat in the blind man's eyes and asked him what he could see. The man replied, "I see people; they look like trees walking around" (Mark 8:24). Then Jesus laid his hands on his eyes again to make him visible. Why did Jesus do this? It wasn't a lack of the ability or the power of healing not working well. No, it must have been the gradual opening of the blind man's faith.

Meanwhile, incases found in Matthew chapter 9, two blind men called out for his mercy with confessions of the Son of David. Jesus touched their eyes and said, "according to your faith let it be done to you" (Matthew 9:29).

When the blind Bartimaeus cried out, "Jesus, Son of David, have mercy on me!" (Mark 10:47), he healed him by saying, "Go, your faith has healed you" (Mark 10:52). It must be because he was already professing his faith in the Messiah, who came as a descendant of David.

In John, the fourth gospel, the author described Jesus as true light: "The true light that gives light to everyone was coming into the world" (John 1:9).It emphasizes that the light of Jesus Christ illuminates the world and falls on each person individually. Just as the light illuminates the whole world and each of us simultaneously, the light of God's Word comes to the whole world and each of us.

These delicate personal touches still overflow with amazing testimonies through the Holy Spirit in the lives of Christians today. Some are clear, some come to us like the morning dew, some are subtle, and some are big and intense. Such testimonies, large or small, confirm the amazing fact that God is guiding our lives rather than the events of our lives. It makes us filled with joy that springs up in our hearts.

The work of the Holy Spirit is accomplished through God's leading grace and faithfulness. It takes more initiative than our wills. God's faithful guidance toward life is the driving force that enables us to pursue such a life. The guidance of the Holy Spirit—that is, God's arbitrary and sovereign choice and guidance—is repeatedly emphasized in Jesus's speech. Leading doesn't mean just considering or giving advice. It's like a fisherman pulling a net. Using the net, the fisherman draws the fish to him. Acceptance of Jesus as Savior cannot be given as moral counsel or persuasion by human hands. It is much more intense and louder than that, and irresistible. It brings out a personal encounter that goes beyond simply knowing or considering God. Everyone who is drawn comes to Jesus. It is the proper response of those who have been led. It is receiving the Word of God, truly knowing that Jesus came from the Father, and believing that the Father sent Jesus Christ (John 17:8).[8]

In encounters and conversations, the personal God engages with us through several channels. The Holy Spirit has various ways of choosing methods for the salvation of one's soul. Through these methods, we can say that God is the one who makes all things possible, and he is always observing and leading us.

The voluntary and proactive guidance of the Holy Spirit, who guides our lives, can be divided into two types: those that occur when we are not aware of them and those we can recognize.

The Word of God does not give us clear directions for our

---

[8] William Hendriksen, *Gospel of John* ((1959) See chapter 6, p. 239.

day-to-day affairs for which there is no special revelation or guidance because we cannot ask every question about the many encounters or events in our lives. And because we do not have clear instructions on the directions we should go, our judgment is based on the Word of God. We choose the direction based on whether it is the path God wants us to take, if it would please God. Such is the guidance, "Therefore be as shrewd as snakes and as innocent as doves"(Matthew 10:17),or, "You are the salt of the earth"(Matthew 5:13),or, "You are the light of the world"(Matthew 5:14) by Jesus, who set the standard and guidance on our lives.

In many cases, the Holy Spirit works through our encounters and environments during our lifetimes. It makes us realize and to confess that it was he who has led us, even when we could not recognize it at those times.

The other is when we recognize the voluntary and initiative drawing of the Holy Spirit. The work of the Holy Spirit, who leads the people belonging to God, sometimes exceeds our expectations. It is arbitrary and proactive; it makes us encounter things that we cannot expect in our usual ways of thinking. We often experience things that happen in ways we never think of and that goes beyond rational thinking or common sense in present circumstances. When we experience God's leading work, we sometimes experience great fear and awe that transcends the emotions felt at the presence of his powerful hand and that sometimes gives us great courage.

This direct or indirect experience or knowledge of the presence of God makes us reverent and opens eyes to the extraordinary and transcendent work of the leading of the Holy Spirit, the highest and more expansive realm than we are. Its infinity is his realm. It opens wide the notion that he is different from us. The fact that God is the highest one, the one who is in control of everything and transcends our human judgment, is something that we cannot fathom. That is why he is most awe-inspiring.

Even in meetings and conversations, the guidance of the Holy

Spirit is difficult to predict from what we can see. We can see his drawing even in unexpected encounters. Such drawing is frequently experienced when evangelizing, such as during severe frustration or even being determined to die by eating poison in his pocket to meet a chance of gospel. We cannot explain other than it being God's will. It also provides comfort and encouragement through a sudden visit or sometimes the experience of a helping hand that meets one's needs in both small and extraordinary cases.

Such signs are difficult to explain without the presence of the Holy Spirit and his leading. Such irresistible drawing can only be called an expression of God's love. These phenomena not only convince us that it is his concrete leading but also strengthens our trust in him.

2. DIALOGUE THAT OPENS EYES

I was walking along Takapuna Beach. New Zealand is an island country, so well-developed beaches are everywhere. At the beach, close to the residential area, many people come out to enjoy a walk when the tide is low. It is a peaceful view. Some people come out to train their physical strength, and some to spend time with their families. Dogs here are compulsorily trained and friendly with people. They accompany their owners and run around to their hearts' content.

When I was taking a stroll along the beach in the late afternoon, I suddenly found a large dog and its owner just entering the beach from a side road not too far away. My eyes were fixed on this site by chance, a dog running in front of its owner, gasping frantically, pulling the leash. I intuitively thought that it was an uneducated dog. There was also white foam around its black, largemouth. I was terrified. I had an ominous feeling that he was running toward me, which made me tense up.

Not surprisingly, when the dog reached the sandy beach, the

owner, apparently struggling with strength, untied the leash, and this terrifying beast sprinted toward me frantically. There was no one around me, so I felt the fear of being targeted. For a moment, my legs tensed, and I knew I had to prepare for an attack. I just wished that this dog would pass me by without incident. Fortunately, the dog passed me and slowed down in front of a little kid, barely walking, twenty meters behind me. It wagged its tail and sniffed. The dog spun around the kid and then ran straight to the cool sea and jumped into the water. What surprised me even more was the reaction of this little kid. It was as if he didn't know about fear yet. large dog over his height came up and licked him. Unafraid, the kid stroked the dog's head; it was as if he had met an old friend. I breathed a sigh of relief.

With this sudden situation, my thoughts went naturally to this dog. What was this dog thinking? The thought crossed my mind that the dog never had any interest in me and the little kid. The interest of this dog was just to run to its heart's content and jump into the seawater. That's right. The dog may have been waiting all day, or even a week, for its owner to take it out. Coming to the open sea, the dog must have wanted to run on the sand to soothe its muscles itching for a good run. Pulling at the leash and dragging its owner, I think, was because the desire to jump into the water was that great.

If I had noticed the dog's thoughts, I would have been able to pass it on by thinking, *It might be so excited*, instead of experiencing fear. Why did I feel afraid? Why did my thoughts only stay on defense and didn't reach this dog's thoughts? This led me to thinking, *Everyone walking on this beach now must be filled with different thoughts*. Suddenly, I found many people walking on different beaches in their worlds, even in the same space. If so, what do their worlds look like? What am I to them? A walk along the beach led to various thoughts.

In our encounters and conversations, it can be said that there are different perspectives of each personality, God, you, and me.

If we look at each of them more schematically, we can break them down into each perspective: the perspective of God toward me and my neighbor, mine to God and neighbor, and neighbor to God and me. These points of view can be found as, "At my sight and at your sight,""On my side and your side, "and "My Father's side and your father's side."This pointed out the limitations of trapped thoughts. For example, "Why is my language not clear to you? Because you are unable to hear what I say" (John8:43), and, "Yet you are looking for a way to kill me, because you have no room for my word" (John 8:37). These three points—what my neighbor's position and opinion are, my position and opinion, and God's intention—constitute a Christian's conversation.

The more we understand others, the more differences we can find. The other person's world is another world completely different from the world I see. Therefore, conversations always need to consider a deeper insight and a balanced approach to the independent personalities. Expanding the perspectives free us from the danger of relying only on self-centered and subjective judgments. It provides a safeguard.

If you engage in dialogue with these three perspectives, you will find more objectivity and composure in the judgment. Furthermore, we will better understand the principles of relationships in our lives and make our conversations much clearer.

We can see that Jesus's conversation was always about showing God and eyeing neighbors. That is the conversation Jesus showed us. In that sense, we are using only one third of the views. The other two thirds are missing. We can say that the important part for Christians to deal with in dialogue is to secure the forgotten perspectives, that is, the perspective of neighbors and God.

For example, while walking down the street, seeing a beggar who had been blind since birth, the disciples asked, "Rabbi, who sinned, this man or his parents, that he was born blind? Who was it that was blind, him because of his sin, or the sins of his parents?" (John 9:2).In the disciples' words, there was no view of

God's work and neighbor in the present situation. The disciples' views were limited to popular scriptural knowledge and gave the impression that they were solving a puzzle in a difficult biblical interpretation. It is a curse to be blind; their eyes were fixed on the source of the blindness. They did not even consider or feel the pain of the miserable life that the blind man faced. They had never expected this moment to show God's glory: "Neither this man nor his parents sinned, but this happened so that the work of God might be displayed in him" (John 9:3).Jesus opened the eyes of the blind. He also opened the disciples' fixed eyes to new perspectives. It was the perspective of God and neighbor(John 9:1–3).

Securing this perspective is also presented in the rebuke of Peter, who tried to persuade Jesus not to take the cross. Although his actions are very human, Jesus rebuked him, saying, "You do not have in mind the concerns of God, but merely human concerns" (Matthew 16:23). He pointed out that Peter missed God's perspective while looking at the same situation. Even amid the crisis of the last arrest, he opened Peter's eyes once more. He corrected the missing of God's sight. When Peter drew his sword and struck one of them, Malchus, in the ear, Jesus ordered, "Put your sword away! shall I not drink the cup that the Father has given me?" (John 18:11).It would not be an exaggeration to say that Jesus's words and conversations were meant to teach the disciples, and even the opposing Jews, to secure both the sight of God and their neighbors.

When Jesus heard the news that Lazarus was terminally ill, he showed his clear view, saying, "This sickness will not end in death. No, it is for God's glory so that God's son may be glorified through it" (John 11:4).

And the courage to break the false precepts of the Jewish Sabbath was also because he had God's point of view. Being able to move to another town, leaving behind the pain of countless sick people, does not mean inhumanity. Rather, it shows that he had God's perspective of fulfilling the eternal plan of salvation. Therefore, even the place and time to act, he could perfectly time according to the Father's eternal plan of salvation.

In many cases, this view of God, which Christians should naturally have, is ignored or lost in daily encounters and conversations. Securing God's perspective when engaging in dialogue is like holding the rudder of a ship. If one misses this key step, the ship goes without direction. When we gain God's perspective, we can see our neighbors' needs.

Therefore, the desirable Christian dialogue is to go beyond my perspective and secure the perspective of God and neighbors. Thus we are able to convey God's Word in a way that suits us. It is a very important way for Christians to develop communication. It is a new attempt to break free from the familiar egocentric instincts and ways of living and the selfish inertia of defense and persuasion for one's benefit and glory.

Indeed, many Christians fail to defend Christianity in their daily encounters and conversations by missing these perspectives. So it will be a great challenge to be constantly trained. It is not only completely incompatible with a self-centered conversational style but also requires a change of habit, which is not easy.

There seems to be no royal road to securing these two lost perspectives other than our relentless efforts to find them out of the self-centered perspective. Until it becomes a habit in meetings and conversations, make an effort to secure a counterpart-centered and God's perspective when having conversations.

A person who gains others' points of view will react differently. How precious it is to have this kind of perspective! Expressions should change and refine. For such people, forgiveness is the ability to understand differences. Tolerance means to embrace differences, moderation is to consider others, and conflict is to express different positions. If help, sharing, and compromise are positive responses, envy, resentment, and anger are negative responses when one does not accept these differences.

An effective conversation depends on how the other person hears and feels not what you feel and say. According to one psychological study, in human communication, the accuracy between what is said and what is heard could be only 17 percent. The response is not taken from me but from the listener, and the changes are mutually reciprocal only when heard in the listener's language. No matter what the truth is, a unilateral declaration or shouting has no effect. So it would be more accurate to say that the delivery of words depends on the listener's ears rather than the speaker's mouth.

When the other person's position is considered and the Word of God is presented precisely to his needs, a response occurs. This change of perspective will change our thinking and language, awaken our spirituality, and allow us to continue the conversation.

Chapter 2
TWO PREREQUISITES FOR DIALOGUE

To LEARN THE CONVERSATION OF JESUS IS NOT SIMPLY TO LEARN the technique or skill of conversation but to learn his life and character. The life of preaching the gospel, the command of Jesus, is our Christian work. That life has the greatest value we should pursue.

1. THE WORD

Above all, the content and goal of Jesus's conversations were to convey God's Word. Suppose the ministry of Jesus Christ was the life of a mediator. In that case, his dialogue would show how he lived as a messenger. This position was emphasized several times. I do not think there is a clearer, more straightforward expression that sums up such a picture: "For I did not speak on my own, but the Father who sent me commanded me to say all that I have spoken. I know that his command leads to eternal life. So whatever I say is just what the Father has told me to say" (John 12: 49–50).

In terms of our conversations, the phrase, "just what the Father has told me to say," seems that it should not be taken literally. Rather, it speaks efficiently so that one can correctly understand the Word of God. It also guides us on how we should approach our neighbors and how to convey the Word of God by adopting a dialogue method.

This perception will change our conversations. Christian life and conversation are always about what pleases God in mind. In other words, it means trying to focus on the role of a messenger and sow the seed of the Word. Functionally speaking, it means restraining my words but trying to find and deliver the perspective based on the Word by converting it accurately and diversely to suit the person with which I want to converse.

Suppose we give authority to our own. In that case, it will attribute to our own authority. But if we speak the perspective based on the Word, it will stand with his authority. We can imagine Jesus's authority. His majesty is hinted at. When the subordinates who went to arrest Jesus after receiving the orders of the religious leader returned empty-handed, one of them remarked, "No one ever spoke the way this man does" (John 7:46).

Jesus placed his authority on the Father by placing himself in a position to hear God's Word directly. He frequently expressed himself as "He who sent" (John 14:24) when speaking to the world. Particularly, his authority in saying, "Very truly I tell you" (John 5:19).Or using such powerful expressions as "Whoever has ears, let him hear" (Matthew 11:15), reflects that he was given independent authority as the Son of God.

We can also find Jesus quoted in various forms of the scripture about truth, propositions, laws of nature, and sayings that others recognize as an authority, like, "As it is written" (Mark 7:6); "Have you never read in the Scriptures?" (Matthew 21:42); "Is it not written in your law?" (John 10:34); "It is written in the prophets" (John 6:45); or, "You are in error because you do not know the Scriptures or the power of God" (Matthew 22:29). Also, the method of adding authority by deriving truth from the citation:"When evening comes, you say, 'It will be fair weather, for the sky is red, and in the morning. 'Today it will be stormy, for the sky is red and overcast. You know how to interpret the appearance of the sky, but you cannot interpret the signs of the times" (Matthew 16:2–3), and so on. When developing a certain logic, these quotations express authority because they have already been verified and have justification. So they were naturally accepted without question.

On the other hand, human speech changes in response to external circumstances. It is variable, constrained, and conditional. Those in power seem to have great weight, but they do not guarantee their words for the long term. It cannot simultaneously satisfy both the near and the far. Judgment is always based on one's interests and honor. The rhetoric attracts men, and the lips are smooth as oil, but they cannot speak good words from corrupt and dirty lips. Hate is well packed, and hostility is concealed, but the viper's mouth kills. The words of saints, great men, and aphorisms are passed down to give us wisdom and impressions in life. Some follow them as their mottos for life. But no expression, advice, or even a good word can give life to the spirit. A lot of wisdom can give us benefits for the flesh but cannot save one's spirit.

Opening a window to others is possible only with the Word of God. We are meant to sow the seed. He grows the seeds of the Word I throw. God gives it a body as he has determined, and to each kind of seed, he gives its own body (1Corinthians 15:38). Correctly applied, the Word becomes a life-changing seed. This attitude is the way to change.

Therefore, the practical ways of conveying his Word in everyday encounters and conversations mean standing on a firm trust with the highest authority and rendering his perspective based on it. That's what we lost in our conversations. We are to reach out our hands to neighbors and open their eyes by delivering the Word by "transforming and applying it to our actual life. This position will open the way for us to respond to the biblical requirement; If anyone speaks, they should do so as one who speaks the very words of God. If anyone serves, they should do so with the strength God provides, so that in all things, God may be praised through Jesus Christ" (1 Peter 4:11).

2. OBEDIENCE

Jesus said, "So whatever I say is just what the Father has told me to say" (John12: 49–50). That is the basic content and goal of the conversation. And, "By myself I can do nothing; I judge only as I hear, and my judgment is just, for I seek not to please myself but him who sent me" (John 5:30), is the attitude of engaging in the conversation that Jesus has shown.

Being unable to do anything as a son does not mean that Jesus is not autonomous and powerless or self-loathing. Rather, he is completely autonomous and independent as the Son, yet it is voluntary obedience to God's higher authority. The prayer at Gethsemane reveals well the meaning of obedience. Jesus wanted to avoid the cup of death and severance of the cross, but he was determined to follow the Father's will. He can choose his good and glory but put himself down and follow the will of God. He was well-acquainted with the glory of man as he also mentioned, "I have come in my Father's name and you do not accept me; but If someone else comes in his own name, you will accept him" (John5:43).

To "put himself down" was not to say that he is ignorant or blind in his judgment. It refers to recognition and obedience to a higher authority.

It is impossible to expect complete obedience from humans because, by nature, humans disobey the Word of God: The mind governed by fresh is hostile to God; it does not submit to God's law, nor can it do so(Romans 8:7). The troubles of the apostle Paul were also noted here:"For I do not do the good I want to do, but the evil I do not want to do—this I keep on doing" (Romans 7:19). He determined to die every day to live an obedient life. In that sense, sanctification is not about reaching a stage where our actions can do well. It is, rather, a process of reaffirming my sinful nature and its appearance in our daily lives by deeply realizing that I am unable to live righteously. Godliness and righteousness do not mean that I can do it but that I cannot do independently.

As Paul added to his religious experiences, he confessed his true self as one who was born without full term, then to less than the saints, and finally to one of the greatest sinners. As far as he found his false self, he was troubled yet found hope in his true self within Christ: For what the law was powerless to do because it was weakened by the fresh, God did by sending his own Son in the likeness of sinful flesh to be a sin offering .(Romans 8:3) Perhaps that is what he meant not to live according to the fresh but live according to the Sprit.

Complete obedience comes with the confession that I cannot do anything independently. Because it is impossible without self-denial, one can only achieve perfect obedience by killing himself (false self) to save himself (true self). To kill the self means rediscovering a lost position in the relationship with God. It is about recovering oneself in a united relationship. My false self will die and be received as my true self again in God.

Oneness begins with lying down through obedience. Lying down is to receive again. The Word of God uncovers all false veneers and reveals our false selves. The false self cannot be seen unless it is reflected in the light of the Word. If I do not stand in front of the mirror of the Word, I cannot see my distorted and false state. The destruction of the false self, which pursued self-interest and glory, begins with seeing one's sinful nature as illuminated by the Word. It states that no one can find his faults before the Word: "Nothing in all creation is hidden from God's sight. Everything is uncovered and laid bare before the eyes of him to whom we must give account" (Hebrews 4:13). It says that no one can hide their sinful appearances: "For our offences are many in your sight, and our sins testify against us. Our offenses are ever with us, and we acknowledge our iniquities" (Isaiah 59:12).

The Word is light. Where there is light, darkness disappears. The finding of light makes us look back on ourselves. The light shakes off all the false envelopes brought about by the severance of the relationship with God and reveals the true self in the relationship. The Word repeatedly encourages us to renounce evil and keep away from it. The more I discover my false self, the more amplified is my reflection with a desire to find my true self. Recognition and discovery of partial self-denial become brighter and brighter under the light and lead to entire self-denial under the guidance of the Holy Spirit.

It comes to be agreed that human thoughts and words cannot be true, and only the Word of God is the eternal unchanging truth and life. Such a life eventually leads to finding the identity of one's true self, coming to deny the false self, making him loath it, and vomiting it out without hesitation.

It seems impossible to deny oneself, but the Holy Spirit takes it along the long journey of life, breaking the chains of sin and leading us to accept, acknowledge, and follow the Word. The work of the Holy Spirit helps us to find our true selves. The emotional decision to live in obedience to God's Word has tremendous power to change our lives.

The destructive power of that force shatters the shell of the self. The false self is like a walnut protected by a hard shell. It cannot escape unless it is broken by the power of the Holy Spirit as if broken with a hammer. However, no one can remove the hidden sinful nature at once. It will not end until the last.

Even in the scorching heat of late summer, the fruits don't look like they will ever grow old. But before the end of autumn, the green fruits quickly get bigger and turn red. As we learn obedience through life's journey, such a life gradually settles in our hearts and moves toward complete obedience. Life's journey in this new world will lead to holistic decisions that entail emotional, rational, and intentional decisions.

God called Abraham at the age of seventy-five. Mistakes and training continued for nearly forty years before he could lay down his only son, Isaac, in front of the altar. To him, offering his son as a burnt offering was harder than killing himself.

Moses was left in the wilderness for forty years. However, even with such humility, he could not completely kill himself. As he hit the rock in front of the people who were supplicating their thirst by putting forth "I" (Numbers20:1–13).

The apostle Paul discovered the truth that he had crucified himself with Jesus Christ on the cross and drew the consciousness that "I have been crucified with Christ and I no longer live, but Christ lives in me. It is not me who lives now, but Christ that lives in me" (Galatians2:20).

Jesus said, "Whoever wants to be my disciple must deny themselves and take up their cross daily and follow me" (Luke 9:23). He also compared it to a farmer plowing a field with a plow: "No one who puts his hand to the plow and looks back is fit for service in the kingdom of God"(Luke 9:62). It's about leaving the old behind and looking forward.

To believe in Jesus Christ is learning to live in the relationship of obedience and to abide in unity. It also refers to a life of absolute personal dependence. I don't think it's necessary to accept this unity in our lives as being too difficult or abstract. Jesus called his disciples to be one: "I have given them the glory that you gave me, that they may be one as we are one" (John17:22). This means that as the disciples lived in conversation with Jesus, we also ask and listen to the Holy Spirit and live in close fellowship with him. It is the same as the Holy Spirit continues to play its role as a counselor for us today, just as the disciples were enough with Jesus alone.

Just as Jesus was a witness to the world about sin, righteousness, and judgment, so is the guidance that the Holy Spirit leads us today. Such communication enables us to sense the Holy Spirit's lead and direction and move forward. It means communicating with him in the amazement of salvation and doing what is pleasing to him. It refers to a life in which my words and actions are connected to him. His joy becomes my joy, and his sorrow becomes my sorrow, as the shepherd knows the sheep, calls them by name, and responds to the sheep's small groans.

Therefore, communication continues every moment of every day. It follows what the Holy Spirit does and consists in receiving the blessings he supplies. As in the parable of the sheep and shepherd, the sheep listen to the shepherd and go in and out of the gate every day, grazing the pasture, resting on the inside, and finding green feed on the outside. It is to experience inner peace by eating the bread of life every day, getting it abundantly, and relying on the shepherd to keep us from real dangers and crises. The thief wants to steal and kill, but Jesus wants the sheep to have life and to have it more abundantly (John 10:7–18).

Jesus described perfect obedience in unity. On the last day, when Jesus was arrested as a high priest that no one could imitate, he repeatedly spoke several times with unparalleled prayer. He desired the disciples to become one:

> My prayer is not for them alone. I also pray for those who will believe in me through their message, that all of them may be one, Father, just as you are in me and I am in you. May they also be in us so that the world may believe that you have sent me. I have given them the glory that you gave me, that they may be one as we are one—I in them and you in me—so that they may be brought to complete unity. Then the world will know that you sent me and have loved them even as you have loved me. (John 17:20–23)

He proclaimed the restoration of a complete relational life through unity. Unity in relationships is ultimate and the final goal for all.

This principle of unity is also the same in the work of the Holy Spirit. Within the words of the Son, the Holy Spirit limits his role and comes to work:

> But when he, the Spirit of truth, comes, he will guide you into all the truth. He will not speak on his own; he will speak only what he hears, and he will tell you what is yet to come. He will glorify me because it is from me that he will receive what he will make known to you. All that belongs to the Father is mine. That is why I said the Sprit will receive from me what he will make known to you. (John 16:13–15)

This relationship in oneness teaches us the way to become one, not speaking arbitrarily, but speaking what is his.The Father-Son relationship, by its very nature, is absolute good and cannot be divided by intimacy. Suffering, torn apart by death on the cross, the Son said on the cross, "My God, my God, why have you forsaken me?" (Matthew 27:46).This screaming is not a scene from a well-planned script but was the pain of severing and destroying real relationships.

The pain of severing the relationship seems to be passed to his Father. Symbolically, the Father, who was so restrained when his Son cried out for a drop of water by saying, "I am thirsty" (John 19:28), has finally lost his focus. The Father tore the veil of the Most Holy in Jerusalem as if it were to rend his heart. And as he could no longer see his Son's suffering, he covered the sky with darkness. His whole body trembled, and the earth couldn't hide his anguish. The stones trembled and were destroyed. The wrath toward death had not yet to come. The plans were ignored, the graves were opened, and the dead were raised to life. It was expressed by a Roman centurion who watched it with fear: "Surely he was the Son of God!" (Matthew 27:54).

Jesus said, "It is finished (*Tetelestai*),"when he died on the cross. The penalty for sin had been paid. It was God's unique solution to the sins of the world. The sting of death is sin, and the power of sin is the law (1 Corinthians 15:56). The atoning blood was paid, and from now on, there will be no more condemnation by the law to whoever believes in him: "But now, by dying to what once bound us, we have been released from the law so that we serve in the new way of the Spirit, and not in the old way of the written code" (Romans 7:6).

The Father's plan is in his love for man and his deep concern for the glorification of his Son. The Father resurrected his Son and glorified him according to his request, making his chosen people one in the Son: "I have glorified it, and will glorify it again" (John12:28).The voice of God was heard by the Son. God, the Father, is glorified through the cross that the Son took up and made one in the Son, his chosen and predestined people.

The Holy Spirit reminds the chosen people of the Word of the Son. He willingly humbles himself to fulfill the work of the Son as a consultant, helper. He descends into the hearts of the people belonging to the Son, reminding them of his words and drawing them into unity in the love of God. Now the Father's will is to believe in the Son. What Jesus Christ has consistently claimed throughout his ministry is to reveal God's plan for eternal life and to trust the Son who does it so that the chosen children may become one and dwell in the glory of the Father.

Relational life is not about being alone but being with God:"My Father, who has given them to me, is greater than all; no one can snatch them out of my Father's hand"(John 10:29). Nothing can break a relationship. Even if I fail to hold his hands, God holds the chosen one with a strong hand. That is the power of relationships. We stumble in weakness, but his faithfulness raises us again. He answers us when we cry out because we are in one.

Just as a seed grows into a big tree, our souls are rebuilt in God, and we share that love with others. Just as the water of a reservoir wets the dry land, so does the thirsty one cool.

If someone desires to transfer the Word of God, he should allow himself to remain only as a messenger and missionary. That is the way of obedience required of us Christians.

Chapter 3
SAY LIKE THIS

Jesus's conversation gives us the strength to dwell in the truth inwardly and makes it easy and natural to preach the gospel outwardly. If yes or no is given as a response to most of our daily lives, Jesus's four-step dialogue evangelism presents an active dialogue method that leads conversation. I think this knowledge and training will take a further step forward in how we talk and contribute significantly to making the most of it.

1. SAY YES OR NO

The only direct mention Jesus makes about our language life is, "All you need to say is simply 'Yes' or 'No'; anything beyond this comes from the evil one" (Matthew5:37).

Many people give advice on the importance of speaking words, but I can't help but marvel at how Jesus can sum up our language life in such a simple word. Why did he say this? He gave this word in connection with the verse not to swear: "Do not swear an oath at all" (Matthew 5:34).That means don't make vain oaths we cannot keep as we cannot be the subjects of our wills. We cannot make even one hair white or black (Matthew 5:36).Even if the rich man who fills the barns wants to eat and play for the rest of his life, if he takes his life that evening, whose wealth belongs to him(Luke12:20)?Even if one says he has the authority to save people and the power to kill, he has no authority to harm them unless God allows(John19:10).The point is that only God is the Lord and subject of judgment. Therefore, do not set yourself up for what you will do, but say what is yes is yes, and what is no is no.

Also, because of fundamental sinful nature, man cannot be good and speak good words. The reason Jesus emphasized many times that "the Word of God is the truth," is because only the Word of God is the life and authority.

It means that only God is the true ruler, the subject of judgment, and the words and thoughts of humans cannot be true. The pride of wanting to be like God is located in man's heart. Without realizing it, he speaks his own words according to his sinful nature. Just as Jesus used harsh words to the Pharisees, saying, "What comes out of a person is what defiles them. For it is from within, out of person's hearts, that evil thoughts come-sexual immorality, theft, murder, adultery, greed, malice, deceit, lewdness, envy, slander, arrogance, and folly. All these evils come from inside and defile a person" (Mark 7:21–23).

Saying yes or no doesn't mean that you should not be reticent or talk too much. Rather, you should be discerning based on God's Word and not judge based on your thoughts and will. Jesus taught that the standard of judgment should be the Word of God, who is the superior authority as it is written, "I have much to say in judgment of you, but he who sent me is trustworthy, and what I have heard I tell the world" (John 8:26).

Jesus's words, "Do not judge," also do not mean that you should not discriminate between right and wrong. It says human criticism is relative:"Do not judge, or you too will be judged. For in the same way you judge others, you will be judged, and with the measure you use, it will be measured to you" (Matthew7:1–2). It means not to criticize and condemn others based on your standards but to discern and render the Word as it is the supreme authority we should seek in our encounters and conversations:"You judge by human standards; I pass judgment on no one. But if I do judge, my decisions are true, because I am not alone. I stand with the Father, who sent me"(John8: 15–16).

This request is also advocated by Peter, who was the chief disciple: "If anyone speaks, they should do so as one who speaks the very words of God. If anyone serves, they should do so with the strength God provides, so that in all things God may be praised through Jesus Christ"(1 Peter 4:11).Isn't that too much of a burden? You might feel it is. However, to express these words more practically, the content of the message is not my or your words, thoughts, or claims but God's Word, or God's perspective based on the Word. It also means that we should be able to confess that the power of helping others is caused by him, not us.

In addition to these hidden meanings, it is also true that these conversational postures bring many benefits. Being able to say yes or no means being bridled. Words can kill or save people's lives; the entire book of James is a warning against this caution. The habit of saying yes or no helps to minimize the risk caused by misunderstandings or unnecessary additions.

Saying yes or no in our conversations is a very accurate and useful expression of our thoughts. We are apt to think that to say a lot is better, and to say yes or no isn't enough to convey our opinions. However, answering the facts that are not exaggerated or dispirited can reduce the room for unnecessary misleading. How inaccurate communication could be when I see others misunderstanding me! So many times we make mistakes in answering bounded by one-sided thoughts without noticing what others are thinking or saying. We speak based on our thinking that they might agree and accept what is said. But in some cases, misunderstanding is led, and their reactions are in the opposite direction. For example, Ototoke Hirotada, the author of *No One's Perfect*, says that when his teacher punished his classmates in school, he was able to gain independence by receiving the same punishment, even though he had no arms or legs. It is also known that physically disabled people may suffer from other people seeing them in that way more than the inconvenience their disability brings.

In dialogues with multiethnic groups, we can experience many striking cultural differences. Our conversations make it easy to ignore the background and environments in which our neighbors grew up. For example, someone's family tradition, financial ability, physical disability, level of development, education, and values are not considered. The same is true of certain religions, formed ideologies, and values of sex, wealth, and honor not only of the other person's internal appearance but also of external changes or circumstances. This is also true in cases of an immediate health problem, event, accident, financial deterioration, and changes in environment, temperament, disposition, character, or special circumstances. In everyday encounters or conversations, the questions of what kind of perspective others have or how they look at it are ignored or far away. We react differently in our thoughts, so individual behaviors are difficult to predict. You can't imagine how different their thoughts are from yours.

The second thing to think about is whether this conversational style is too defensive or passive. It's probably not. A clear expression of yes or no is used not only as a function of self-defense but also as an active means of revealing the glory of God. It is not easy to answer yes or no; sometimes it requires great courage. For example, it is not easy to say no when it goes against the intention of the group or organization in cases of unfair treatment or when illegality is imposed. Rejection is related to the severance of relationships or disadvantages. However, saying no does not necessarily mean that the relationship is broken. Rather, you can expect the other person's reaction or treatment and gain support through such a process. Once you say no, you will be ridiculed the first time. But the second time they will not ignore and the third will be heeded. There is not much need to shout. Yes or no is enough.

Also, it would be helpful if you think that one thing at a time is enough. It is impossible to spread the gospel all at once. As you can see in the ministry of Jesus, he gave his disciples the Word from time to time during the three-and-a-half-year-period. The more we meet, the closer we get to what we are trying to render. I remember playing the game Twenty Questions. It is a game to determine what the someone has in mind within twenty guesses. The other person can answer only with yes or no. If we answer yes or no to everyone we meet in our daily lives, they will gradually come to know the gospel. Jesus taught his disciples in this way. After that, leave the remaining in God's hands. Jesus entrusted all his disciples into our Father's hands during his final prayer. And he could say, "It is finished." We also need to do what is given to us in the ministry and leave the rest in his hands. It will be enough for us to do what we can deliver.

Just like a play is a series of acts, it is important how the actors express the will of the director, whatever the newly given environments are. I think acts that reveal the glory of him do not always depend on how far we should go and what things we should do, but rather, on how we respond to what comes to us. The record of the Bible is the history of reactions of faith-minded individuals amid upheaval and change. Sometimes the background can be a peaceful everyday life and sometimes bloody as during war. There are people living in poverty to abundance, from oppression to freedom, and from suffering to overcoming. Whatever the circumstances of our lives, our choices depend on whether we answer yes or no.

Hence, feelings of guilt make it hard to say yes or no. The lust for money, sex, and fame that arises from inside is difficult to overcome for everyone. It is shameful to say yes or no to someone when you can't do it properly. Word of man expresses his faith and character. Therefore, it is also the reason Christians should strive to maintain holy lives so that there is no spot or blemish in his life:"So then, dear friends, since you are looking forward to this, make every effort to be found spotless, blameless and at peace with him"(2 Peter 3:14).

2. USE MARSHAL

Eternal life is the most fundamental desire of human beings that resembles the image of God. The longing for salvation is hidden in everyone. Though these longings seem to be hidden and ignored, they cannot be completely hidden. That longing cries out to our souls; the cries turn into screams. Death reminds everyone of this fact. So it is sublime and dignified. It is also the most powerful warning and invitation to awaken everyone to God. The basis on which we present God to our neighbors who neither know nor believe is that they already have the knowledge to know it and are under the authority and judgment of the Creator. The longing for eternal life is the trace of God's love that awakens the sleeping spirit. And it is also the most fundamental resource.

Our daily lives consist of countless conversations. According to one study, people speak an average of between seven thousand and twenty thousand words a day, which is considered necessary for mental health. Most of our daily conversations are focused on the issue of flesh. Just as Jesus pointed out, it is mostly related to what to eat, drink, and wear. However, suppose our conversations began with the flesh and ended with the flesh. In that case, we miss the opportunity to convey God's message and save the spirit. The flesh is the basis for saving the spirit. Jesus said, "the Spirit gives life; the flesh counts for nothing. The words I have spoken to you—they are full of the Spirit and life" (John 6:63).

We can see many cases when Jesus led from the matter of the flesh to a conversation that saved the spirit and lives. He introduced eternal life with simple barley bread and water, which led to a spiritual fullness and everlasting spring that never becomes thirsty. The affairs of the flesh are the foundation for saving the Spirit.

The following conversations introduce how Jesus showed God in the cases of Nicodemus and the Samaritan woman longing for eternal life and salvation, and Martha, who was grieving before the death of Lazarus. It was also the case when Jesus faced threats, including murder.

As a way of conveying truth, Jesus used veiled words at the beginning of his conversations that answered questions and had deep spiritual meanings. This unique technique was named "marshal" by the commentator William Hendriksen. If the parable is an enumeration, the marshal is given as an answer with spiritual meaning in the immediate context.[9]

Marshal is a unique way of expression to derive the Spirit from the flesh. It is a method of delivering the type from antitype, conveying the substance from the illusion. This intriguing statement makes a person realize what was said only after hearing the whole story. For example, "Very truly I tell you, no one can see the kingdom of God unless they are born again" (John 3:3). Or, "Very truly I tell you, unless you eat the flesh of the Son of Man and drink his blood, you have no life in you. Whoever eats my flesh and drinks my blood has eternal life and I will raise them up at the last day" (John 6:53).

Appropriate use of these marshals makes it efficient to convey the Word of God while leading the conversation. Marshal is primarily a topic of conversation and arouses curiosity at the starting of the conversation. A supplementary explanation is added to explain more about marshal easily, two or three times if needed, and mainly utilizes onsite materials such as water, wind, bread, and food.

When Jesus went up to Jerusalem for the Jewish Passover, he

---

[9] William Hendriksen, *Gospel of John* (1959) A marshal is a paradoxical saying, a veiled and pointed remark often in the form of a riddle. See p. 124.

threw away the burial sacrifices, overturned the money changers' tables, and sanctified the temple. Marshal was given in reply:"destroy this temple, and I will raise it in three days" (John 2:19). The words "destroy the temple," allow for two interpretations. It can be said to mean architecture and refer to the human body. In saying that the Jews built it for forty-six years, it can refer to the temple, but it can also be seen as the body in which the soul resides. The Jewish view relates to a temple, so the words, "destroy this temple, and I will raise it again in three days" (John 3:19) will plunge them into a pit they do not know. The part where Jesus said he would, "raise it," in three days can also be interpreted as rebuilding the temple or the resurrection of the body—the temple he had spoken of was his body—and the birth of a new temple, the church that worships in Spirit and truth as a result.

Marshal is also the ladder between reality and belief. Where the Word cannot reach, marshal works. These marshals can be found in many places. When King Herod was about to kill Jesus, he said, "Go tell that fox, 'I will keep on driving out demons and healing people today and tomorrow, and on the third day I will reach my goal'" (Luke 13:32). "In a little while, you will see me no more, and then after a little while you will see me," and, "Because I am going to the Father" (John 16:17). Marshal becomes an aid to delivering the Word better. Marshal can be a valuable tool for conveying spiritual meaning in various fields. As we can see from the examples, it greatly influences raising each person's faith to illuminate the light and introduce truth and life.

The following examples are conversations that devote a relatively large space to the fourth gospel. We can see that these dialogues have a unique pattern. Although the circumstances are different, the way they unfold is the same. Each takes the form of a marshal with a supplementary explanation, rebuke, and application with an invitation. This pattern is seen in conversations with Nicodemus, the Samaritan woman, Martha, and with the Jews immediately after the miracle of the five loaves of bread and two fishes. It is even seen in the conflict situation at the Feast of Tabernacles.

The summarized diagram that follows illustrates the pattern well.

	Nicodemus	Samaritan Woman	Conversation with Jews	Conflict at the Tabernacles
Marshal	Unless born again, cannot see kingdom of God.	If you ask him, he will give you living water.	Work for food that endures to everlasting life.	The truth will set you free.
React	Negative: How can I be born again?	Negative: Are you higher than Jacob?	Murmuring	Rebellious: Never been a slave.
Supplementary Explanation	Must be born of water and Spirit	The water I give will never thirst.	It is God's work to believe in me.	Who commits a sin is a slave to sin.
React	Skeptical: How is it possible?	Misunderstood physically: Let me not come to draw water.	Negative: Are you greater than Moses? Then give me the Bread of Life.	Resistant: My father is Abraham.
Rebuke	Do you not know as an Israeli teacher?	Bring your husband.	You see me, but do not believe me.	You are trying to kill me, the one who spoke the truth.
React	Silence.	Silence (no husband).	Quarrel: How did he come down from heaven?	Violent quarrels: We were not born of harlotry.
Application and Invitation	Those who seek the truth come to the light.	I am the one who speaks to you.	Whoever eats my bread and drinks my blood will live forever.	If you keep my word, you will never see death.
React	Testimony and dedication.	Joy and evangelism.	Denial.	Violence: turning to stone.
Field Material	The wind and the brass serpent of the wilderness.	Wall and the temple.	Bread, flesh, and blood.	Freedom and slavery.

Marshal and Supplementary explanation

A marshal's purpose is to make first-time listeners think and raise curiosity, leading to deeper conversations. It contains a rather unrealistic contradiction hidden behind a veil. But it reveals spiritually deep truths that are realized as soon as someone hears the whole thing. The marshal unleashes and leads one to a spiritual perspective. At some point, everything suddenly comes to light.

Although Jesus used this expression in many places, individuals and audiences reacted differently. Some listened earnestly, but some were always negative and hostile, as seen in his conversations with Jews. Those who did not understand the truth criticized him for being vague or deceptive.

Marshal was used mainly to reveal Jesus's identity. We can see that it was very effective in introducing and delivering content. Marshal is seen in almost all conversational forms. Jesus gave it at the beginning of the conversation, and it aroused the listeners' spiritual curiosity. Supplementary explanations followed, and reprimands were given according to the listeners' reactions. And without exception, Jesus gave an invitation to eternal life.

When given a marshal, it first arouses curiosity among listeners. But they if they misunderstand it, miss the meaning of the truth. Then it gives a more detailed, supplementary explanation to help the listeners understand. Sometimes supplementary explanations are omitted or duplicated.

Rebuke and Invitation

In Jesus's dialogic evangelism, unlike other known evangelism methods, reproof was given at an appropriate level according to the listener's reaction during the conversation and was used in the form of a calling for an awakening. Depending on the degree of reaction and intensity, it stimulated the stiffened spirits, whether increased step by step or duplicated. After that, it allowed the presentation of the gospel unilaterally. Eventually, it became a leading conversation topic.

The gospel is God's desire to save lives. It is also a word of warning; one should not underestimate the effectiveness of rebuke or awareness or reproof. The failure of daily evangelism to bear fruit is often caused by overlooking the effectiveness of these remedies.

Rebuke is a very important function in waking up the opponent, and it leads to a choice. These reproofs encourage or convince listeners to turn to the truth. A rebuke works often more effectively than ten gentle persuasions. Therefore, it should not be given excessively. Instead, it can be given in stages according to the reaction or resistance of the listener. The rebuke is based on the facts that everyone already knows God, and deep in their hearts, there is a longing for eternal life.

If we look at the cases in which reproofs were given to the disciples Nathanael, Philip, or the disciples going to Emmaus, they are very light. To Nicodemus, "You are Israel's teacher, and do you not understand these things?" (John 3:10). And to the Samaritan woman, "Go, call your husband and come back" (John 4:16). Even in the Jewish conversation, just after the great miracle of five loaves of bread and two fish, light rebukes were given for self-awareness, saying, "But as I told you, you have seen me, and still you do not believe"(John 6:36). However, to those whose party was opposed, it was given more weight as there was no way to escape it: "As it is, you are looking for a way to kill me, a man who has told you the truth that I heard from God. Abraham did not do such things. You are doing the works of your own father"(John 8:40–41)."You belong to your father, the devil, and you want to carry out your father's desire" (John 8:44)."Yet because I tell the truth, you do not believe me!" (John 8:45)."But I honor my Father and you dishonor me" (John 8:49), and so on.

I need to add the following story simultaneously to avoid

evangelism's misuse because in many cases, it happens. Evangelism is the spreading of God's love to our neighbors in the presence and power of the Holy Spirit. The action must be in the love of God. It must not have other motive or purpose nor be instrumentalized for the benefit of oneself or the group. It should be presented with no additional conditions or demands beyond the scope of its essence, and it should accord with the Word of God and justify the religious action. Wrong motives may block God's intentions and come to work against him.

I remember the story of an evangelist. During a family visitation service, the evangelist severely scolded the husband, a church member, to make him repent for his hidden sins. The bewildered husband confessed his adultery during worship as he was afraid of God. After the service was over, the wife fought with her husband, eventually leading to their separation. Surprisingly, there are many similar cases. The church seems to be no exception. Coercion, a false sense of authority, class consciousness, and unbiblical application exist. It is a fact that the sermons of heretical cults have resulted in intimidation and horror. It would say that the application is like a scalpel on an operating table. When used properly, it brings change and life. But when used incorrectly, it kills. If applied excessively or more than necessary, it often creates other problems and can easily cause another incident.

Finally, invitations are given without exception. It would not be an exaggeration to say that all the words of Jesus have a purpose in invitations. Regardless of conformity or strong resistance, without exception, the invitation to eternal life is given at the end of the conversation. Invitations are given with application, even in conflict situations. We can even say rebukes are also for the giving of invitations.

Only the conversations with Nicodemus and Martha are mentioned here for space reasons. Conversations with the Samaritan woman, with the Jews, and the Feast of Tabernacles

(John 8:30–59) are included in the appendix and organized separately.

Let's start with Nicodemus.

> Now there was a Pharisee, a man named Nicodemus, who was a member of the Jewish ruling council.
>
> He came to Jesus at night and said, "Rabbi, we know that you are a teacher who has come from God. For no one could perform the signs you are doing if God were not with him."
>
> Jesus replied, "Very truly I tell you, no one can see the kingdom of God unless they are born again."
>
> "How can someone be born when they are old?" Nicodemus asked. "Surely they cannot enter a second time into their mother's womb to be born!"
>
> Jesus answered, "Very truly I tell you, no one can enter the kingdom of God unless they are born of water and the Spirit.
>
> "Flesh gives birth to flesh, but the Spirit gives birth to spirit.
>
> "You should not be surprised at my saying, 'You must be born again.' The wind blows wherever it pleases. You hear its sound, but you cannot tell where it comes from or where it is going. So it is with everyone born of the Spirit."
>
> "How can this be?" Nicodemus asked.

"You are Israel's teacher," said Jesus, "and do you not understand these things?

"Very truly I tell you, we speak of what we know, and we testify to what we have seen, but still you people do not accept our testimony.

"I have spoken to you of earthly things and you do not believe; how then will you believe if I speak of heavenly things?

"No one has ever gone into heaven except the one who came from heaven—the Son of Man.

"Just as Moses lifted up the snake in the wilderness, so the Son of Man must be lifted up, that everyone who believes may have eternal life in him.

"For God so loved the world that he gave his one and only Son, that whoever believes in him shall not perish but have eternal life.

"For God did not send his Son into the world to condemn the world, but to save the world through him.

"Whoever believes in him is not condemned, but whoever does not believe stands condemned already because they have not believed in the name of God's one and only Son.

"This is the verdict: Light has come into the world, but people loved darkness instead of light because their deeds were evil.

"Everyone who does evil hates the light, and will not come into the light for fear that his deeds will be exposed.

"But whoever lives by the truth comes into the light, so that it may be seen plainly that what he has done has been done in the sight of God."(John 3:1–21)

A. CONVERSATION WITH NICODEMUS

Greetings: "Rabbi, we know that you are a teacher who has come from God. For no one could perform the signs you are doing if God were not with him" (John 3:2).

Nicodemus was a devout man who decided to give his whole life to God. He belonged to the conservative Pharisees, was a member of the Sanhedrin, and a Jewish religious leader. Like those who devoted themselves to religious life in general, he was also a man who learned and taught scripture and set out in search of the truth. His long years of religious life and social position look like a man who had everything. Nicodemus's need was the answer to salvation and eternal life.

He came to Jesus personally at night to seek answers to his serious concerns, despite his position. His polite greeting that "the sign comes from God" gives us a glimpse into the idea that this expression contains the confession that there is a limit to salvation by the creed of the Pharisees (pietism), to which he belongs.

Marshal: "Very truly I tell you, no one can see the kingdom of God unless they are born again" (John 3:3).

It is not the usual way of reciprocating greetings from others. This kind of count-centered conversation goes beyond the usual greetings and formalities. It makes the listener approach his request directly. It's like having a casual conversation with old friends. Jesus gave his greeting and immediately threw a marshal, which quickly aroused curiosity.

Reaction: "How can someone be born when they are old?" "Surely they cannot enter a second time into their mother's womb to be born!" (June 3:4).

This question is a rhetorical one used by the Pharisees at that time. Although it is superficially very negative, it contains curiosity. He is now interpreting it physically.

Supplementary Explanation: "Very truly I tell you, no one can enter the kingdom of God unless they are born of water and the Spirit. Flesh gives birth to flesh, but the Spirit gives birth to spirit. You should not be surprised at my saying, 'You must be born again'" (John 3:5).

For Nicodemus, "water" would have immediately been recognized as referring to John the Baptist's water baptism, spreading beyond the religious category to social problems. At that time, the Pharisees had a sense of crisis as John the Baptist's water baptism threatened their existing legitimacy. And as he started to be thought of as the Messiah in the eyes of the people, they formally asked him who he was in a series of attempts to discredit him, including sending him to an investigative team. But the idea of being born again by the Holy Spirit sounded strange to Nicodemus. "It was a time when there was no concept of baptism with the Holy Spirit, so along with the authoritative expression of Jesus, doubts continue with 'how?' His attention is focused on introducing the new Holy Spirit.

"Flesh gives birth to flesh, but the Spirit gives birth to spirit" (John 3:6). The supplementary explanation brightened him, who did not understand the parable of being born again. It is saying that fleshly conditions or achievements cannot revive the spirit, though he doesn't realize he is being led. Here we can see the leading dialogue of Jesus.

Wind, a field material, was used to explain the Holy Spirit. How could he explain the Holy Spirit so easily? It is amazing how simple wind has turned into an excellent teaching tool. Just as the wind does not blow according to anyone's will, the Holy Spirit reveals God's sovereignty, which moves independently and arbitrarily.

Reaction: "How can this be?" (John 3:9).

How? Doubts continued. For him, this is a natural reaction. It makes Nicodemus find himself deeply in spiritual ignorance.

Rebuke: "You are Israel's teacher," said Jesus, "and do you not understand these things? Very truly I tell you, we speak of what we know, and we testify to what we have seen, but still you people do not accept our testimony.

"I have spoken to you of earthly things and you do not believe; how then will you believe if I speak of heavenly things? "

At this moment, a light rebuke to he who has fallen into a state of spiritual numbness, urges him to awaken to the truth. "As a teacher in Israel, do you not know these things? But still you people do not accept our testimony. I have spoken to you of earthly things and you do not believe, how then will you believe if I speak of heavenly things?" (The same can be found in the conversation with the Samaritan woman described in the next chapter. It was given for spiritual awakening through the inner illumination to "Go, call your husband and come back") (John 4:16).

The supplementary explanation goes back to his first salutation, where the word "we" is used in contrast. Nicodemus's, "what we know," is the knowledge that comes from men. Still, Jesus's contrasting, "what we have seen," is that God's eternal plan of salvation is beyond any doubt and the signs you said will confirm it. What we see leads to the proclamation of even greater heavenly works. What is the work of heaven? A supplementary explanation continues to Nicodemus: "No one has ascended into heaven except the one who came down from heaven, that is, the Son of Man" (John 3:13). Jesus awakens the fact that he has come down from heaven—that is, incarnation—and reveals the secrets of heaven.

Application: Just as Moses lifted the snake in the wilderness, so the Son of Man must be lifted up, so everyone who believes may have eternal life in him (John 3:14).

The example of the brass serpent incident is an opportunity to brighten Nicodemus's dark spiritual eyes instantly. Many scribes read this incident, and Nicodemus, the scribe, must have been well aware of it. However, the perspective of seeing it as a Messiah that saves humankind is first revealed now by Jesus Christ himself. The supreme love of God is revealed in the parable of the bronze serpent hanging on a pole, the culmination of God's supreme love revealed by the death through the crucifixion:"Just as Moses lifted up the snake in the wilderness, so the Son of Man must be lifted up, that everyone who believes may have eternal life in him" (John 3:14).

Here, Moses' brass serpent incident is used as excellent material for the explanation that opens the eyes of Nicodemus, who still does not understand. (In the case of the bronze serpent in the Pentateuch [Numbers 21] of Moses, the people of Israel sinned against God, fiery serpents bit them in the desert, and many died. But God, who heard Moses' prayers, opened a way to live, saying, "Make a snake and put it up on a pole; anyone who is bitten can look at it and live" [Numbers 21:8],and that is what happened.) This citation must have been a very strong corroborating message for Nicodemus, who studied and taught the Torah daily as a scribe. (Just like when John the Baptist, who had identified himself as "the voice of one calling in the desert," asked a skeptical question to Jesus, "Are you the one who is to come, or should we expect someone else?"[Luke 7:19]).Jesus's reply brightened his eyes and put an end to doubts by quoting the scripture of the prophet Isaiah: "Then will the eyes of the blind be opened and the ears of the deaf unstopped" (Isaiah 35:5). This brass serpent incident written in the Law of Moses, which he regarded as the highest, was an irresistible authority. In other words, just as everyone who saw the bronze serpent with the belief would live, it is also true that everyone who believes in the atoning death of the only begotten Son will not perish but have eternal life. A new authority that directly counters that salvation is given by faith through the grace of God instead of the Pharisees' creed that works give salvation. In the case of the brass serpent, he must have seen the way of God's wonderful plan. Nicodemus's constant questions of how is no more.

For Nicodemus, this parable must have quenched his spiritual thirst. It is a completely different path from the Pharisees' creed. He finally realized the truth that was hidden in the first greeting. Man cannot achieve salvation on their own by doing perfect good. There is no way to break the chain of sin. The only way for Nicodemus, who fell into self-contradiction, to escape is not through the Law of Moses but through faith in Christ's atonement for the cross, as in the case of the brass serpent.

Invitation: "Everyone who does evil hates the light, and will not come into the light for fear that his deeds will be exposed.

"But whoever lives by the truth comes into the light, so that it may be seen plainly that what he has done has been done in the sight of God"(John 3:20–21).

Jesus's polite invitation is being given to him; "whoever lives by the truth comes into the light, so that it may be seen plainly that what he has done has been done in the sight of God." (John 3:1–21)

Jesus quenched Nicodemus's thirst by using the field materials wind and water, and quotations of brass serpents to suit him who heard. Two and a half years after this meeting, looking at Jesus on the cross, he discovered that the brass serpent was a type of Christ and that he is the Christ.

Nicodemus's change is reflected in his convictions. The Sanhedrin, to which he belonged—and the highest religious, administrative, and judicial body in Judea at the time—defended Jesus at a crucial point in their decision to kill him. His bold act of bringing a hundred pounds of a mixture of myrrh and incense to the funeral of Jesus, despite the worst-case scenario of losing everything, was very solemn and brave and spoke of his confession of faith.[10]

We'll now take a look at Martha.

> Now a man named Lazarus was sick. He was from Bethany, the village of Mary and her sister Martha. (This Mary, whose brother Lazarus now lay sick, was the same one who poured perfume on the Lord and wiped his feet with her hair.) So the sisters sent word to Jesus, "Lord, the one you love is sick."When he heard this, Jesus said, "This sickness will not end in death. No, it is for God's glory so that God's Son may be glorified through it."Now Jesus loved Martha and her sister and Lazarus. So when he heard that Lazarus was sick, he stayed where he was two more days, and then he said to his disciples, "Let us go back to Judea.""But Rabbi, "they said, "a short while ago the Jews there tried to stone you, and yet you are going back there?"Jesus answered, "Are there not twelve hours of daylight? A man who walks in the daytime will not stumble, for he sees by this world's light. It is when he walks by night that they stumble, for they have no light."After he had said this, he went on to tell them, "Our friend Lazarus has fallen asleep; but I am going there to wake him up."His disciples replied, "Lord if he sleeps, he will get better."Jesus had been speaking of his death, but his disciples thought he meant natural sleep. So then he told them plainly, "Lazarus is dead, and for your sake I am glad I was not there, so that you may believe. But let us go

---

[10] William Hendrickson, *Gospel of John* (1959) See chapter 3, pp. 129–152.

to him."Then Thomas (also known as Didymus) said to the rest of the disciples, "Let us also go, that we may die with him."On his arrival, Jesus found that Lazarus had already been in the tomb for four days. Now Bethany was less than two miles from Jerusalem, and many Jews had come to Martha and Mary to comfort them in the loss of their brother. When Martha heard that Jesus was coming, she went out to meet him, but Mary stayed at home."Lord, "Martha said to Jesus, "if you had been here, my brother would not have died. But I know that even now God will give you whatever you ask."Jesus said to her, "Your brother will rise again."Martha answered, "I know he will rise again in the resurrection at the last day."Jesus said to her, "I am the resurrection and the life. He who believes in me will live, even though he dies; and whoever lives and believes in me will never die. Do you believe this?""Yes, Lord, "she replied, "I believe that you are the Messiah, the Son of God, who is to come into the world."After she had said this, she went back and called her sister Mary aside. "The Teacher is here, "she said, "and is asking for you."When Mary heard this, she got up quickly and went to him.

Now Jesus had not yet entered the village, but was still at the place where Martha had met him. When the Jews who had been with Mary in the house, comforting her, noticed how quickly she got up and went out, they followed her, supposing she was going to the tomb to mourn there. When Mary reached the place where Jesus was and saw him, she fell at his feet and said, "Lord, if you had been here, my brother would not have died." When Jesus saw her weeping, and the Jews who had come along with her also weeping, he was deeply moved in spirit and troubled. "Where have you laid him?" he asked. "Come and see, Lord, "they replied. Jesus wept. Then the Jews said, "See how he loved him!"

But some of them said, "Could not he who opened the eyes of the blind man have kept this man from dying?" Jesus, once more deeply moved, came to the tomb. It was a cave with a stone laid across the entrance. "Take away the stone, "he said. "But, Lord, "said Martha, the sister of the dead man, "by this time there is a bad odor, for he has been there four days."

Then Jesus said, "Did I not tell you that if you believe, you will see the glory of God?"

So they took away the stone. Then Jesus looked up and said, "Father, I thank you that you have heard me.

"I knew that you always hear me, but I said this for the benefit of the people standing here, that they may believe that you sent me." When he had said this, Jesus called in a loud voice, "Lazarus, come out!" The dead man came out, his hands and feet wrapped with strips of linen, and a cloth around his face. Jesus said to them, "Take off the grave clothes and let him go."

Therefore many of the Jews who had come to visit Mary, and had seen what Jesus did, believed in him. But some of them went to the Pharisees and told them what Jesus had done. (John 11:1–46)

B. CONVERSATION WITH MARTHA

In summary, it is as follows.

Greetings: "Lord, the one you love is sick" (John 11:3).

Martha first met Jesus when she heard that he was passing by. She invited him to her house and served food. A woman who provided food and rest and her sister, Mary, and brother, Lazarus, maintained a close relationship with Jesus and were loved. It seems that Jesus often stopped by this house to rest when he was near Jerusalem. Martha understood and followed Jesus's ministry as a disciple. When her brother became seriously ill, Martha urgently sent someone to report this to Jesus when he was in Jerusalem, a few miles from Bethany. She only conveyed Lazarus's sickness, and no request was made separately, which shows that their relationship with Jesus was so close that they did not need to give any detailed explanations as expressed as a loved one.

Marshal: "This sickness will not end in death. No, it is for God's glory so that God's Son may be glorified through it" (John 11:4).

This marshal may also have been passed on to her through a messenger sent by sisters. That fact is reflected in Martha's conversation as well.

Reaction: "If you had been here, my brother would not have died. But I know that even now God will give you whatever you ask" (John 11:21).

While waiting, her brother dies, and the funeral is held. When she meets Jesus, she has a grudge as he comes to her three days after her brother's death. It was difficult to expect anything now, three days later. Nevertheless, it shows that she is holding on to some possibility in the content of Jesus's foretelling.

Supplementary Explanation: "Your brother will rise again" (John 11:23).

Jesus speaks clearly.

Reaction: "I know he will rise again in the resurrection on the last day" (John 11:24).

Martha is still unable to accept these words. Her confession shows she knows that there will be a resurrection at the end. But now, she is unable to see Jesus's wonderful plan.

Rebuke: "I am the resurrection and the life. The one who believes in me will live, even though they die; and whoever lives and believes in me will never die. Do you believe this?" (John 11:25–26).

Jesus takes her faith, she "knows," one step further with a light rebuke. From knowing of the resurrection on the last day, she also must be made to believe that Lazarus, even though he had died three days ago, could also be raised to life. It requires the belief that Jesus is the resurrection and the life.

Reaction: "I believe that you are the Messiah, the Son of God, who was to come into the world" (John 11:27).

Martha understands these words as the resurrection on the last day and believes it will be true on that final day. Even though Martha's confession of this resurrection has progressed from know to believe, it is not yet accepted as a reality when looking at her words and actions. When Jesus asks to remove the stone blocking the tomb, it is shown that Martha's belief is not strong enough to support the idea that Jesus is the Messiah and that her brother will rise again in the final resurrection. Even though she has faith in the resurrection, she missed the power of Emmanuel; God is with us. Even repeated expressions show no expectations of further progress.

Rebuke: "Take away the stone" (John 11:39).

The conversation with Martha continued. When Martha

went home and then returned Jesus went to the stone-lined tomb and said, "Take away the stone" (John11:39). He gives directions and rebukes Martha directly, who still cannot accept it as fact. These words (like the saying to a Samaritan woman, "Go, call your husband and come back" [John 4:16]) make her examine herself in silence. We can assume that Jesus's eyes are focused on Martha to build up her belief.

Reaction: "But, Lord, by this time, there is a bad odor, for he has been there four days" (John 11:39).

Martha's reaction remains negative despite repeated rebukes. Her eyes focused on the corpse, which must have been decomposed, and she had not been able to focus on anything else.

Application: "Did I not tell you that if you believe, you will see the glory of God?" (John 11:40).

Application was given as form of a direct rebuke for not believing in reality.

Invitation: "Father, I thank you that you have heard me.

"I knew that you always hear me, but I said this for the benefit the people standing here, that they may believe that you sent me" (John 11:41–42).

Jesus raises Lazarus from the dead four days later. The invitation is given in the form of a prayer to all who have been surrounded by it.[11]

We can find the same pattern of evangelism. Here, Jesus is raising Martha's faith. It seems to be why he added three calls for a rebuke to her hesitancy, which she could not accept as factual. If the previous Nicodemus and Samaritan woman cases used onsite materials—that is, wind and water—the fact of death itself is taken as onsite material here. This approach allows a different approach from Mary's and Martha's many existing thematic interpretations. For example, if Martha is outward and focused on serving, Mary is treated as a person who broke the alabaster,

---

[11] William Hendriksen, *Gospel of John*(1959) See chapter20, pp. 447–458.

loves the Word of Jesus, and has a religious superiority. Or as some stress, it is the importance of worship and devotion in the church.

In the text, it is clear that Martha, not Mary, is the central character who needs to raise her faith.

Then, is it possible to introduce this evangelism method into our encounters and conversations practically?

We can't be like Jesus. In the case of the Samaritan woman, Jesus showed omniscience by knowing everything about her life. In conversations with Nicodemus and the Jews, the miracle was presupposed. And in the case of Martha, the power of resurrection to raise the dead shows a divine power that no one can imitate. However, it is self-evident that Jesus's four-step evangelism method is the most effective evangelism method. The effects of this method suggest that we need to introduce it into our conversations and actively utilize it.

But in utilizing this method, one problem remains. Namely, where can we find marshal? Yes, it can never come as great as it did by Jesus. However, we can find the right words at the right time through wisdom from the Holy Spirit and careful observation. Also, it doesn't seem like it should be too difficult for us to find. This is because the words of God that we know about are all intriguing or mysterious to those who have not heard the gospel. The gospel itself is a hidden mystery. Every truth in the Bible is marshal itself. Also, it would not be too much to say that all of Jesus's conversations and teachings are marshal offerings. (Refer to the field materials and field training in chapter 4.)

I have a personal anecdote that relates to this topic. While I was taking care of my mother at hospital, a woman in the same room had severe stage-4 lung cancer. She was waiting for death more than the hope of life. This woman was in her late fifties, intelligent, and had a calm personality. One day I suddenly felt the need in my heart to convey the gospel and give hope to her. I said, "Madam, if I were you, I would pray for healing and hold on to the hope of heaven." That was a marshal. On hearing this, she became curious and showed interest. I added that Jesus raised the dead and the hopeless (a supplementary explanation).

The lady said that her daughter had asked her to go to church several times. Still, she could not decide because her sister-in-law belonged to a strange denomination and urged her to attend their assembly meetings as well. But she was negative about this proposal because the way her sister-in-law was insisting felt strange and showed an abnormal way of life. She thought that if she went to her daughter's church, it could be troublesome and uncomfortable (react) regarding her sister-in-law.

I emphasized that "On the last day, we all shall stand alone before God, and the salvation is a matter of mine, not others" (a rebuke).She was quiet for a while. She seemed to be deeply affected by hearing this. I added that everyone who sought God would find Him (an application). When I suggested prayer for her, she got up from the bed and sat down, even though it was quite uncomfortable for her to move. She put her hands flat together and said, "I pray for the first time in my life. Can I do this way?"

I saw her desire to accept Jesus and the hope for eternal life and healing. I said to her, "God looks at the heart and finds those who seek him" (the invitation).I was amazed at her positive response. That Sunday, we worshipped together at a church affiliated with the hospital. I introduced her to a female evangelist in charge of the hospital ministry. I later heard that she attended the worship services without fail. Her confession that she accepted Jesus Christ is has the most precious value even if her life ends. I sincerely hope that she recovers. Meanwhile, her unstable situation made it easier to meet God. Jesus's four-step evangelism made it easy to have valuable encounters and conversations.

Chapter 4
USE THE FIELD

THERE IS NO OTHER PLACE WHERE COMMUNICATION IS BETTER than the meeting site. An indirect opportunity—seminar, sermon, lecture, meeting, and so on—takes time to introduce and requires explanations. It could be cumbersome and difficult to ensure the accuracy of the transmission due to errors that may come because of this method of communication. While the scene of personal interaction is different, it's direct because the other person's point of view and needs come right out. It's easy to see facial expressions, moods, emotions, and feelings that can hardly be conveyed through text messages or phone calls.

It would be no exaggeration to say that Jesus always applied the truth onsite. So the words spoken in the field are alive. It cannot be comparable to teaching at a desk. Even when he revealed his identity (the Seven Great I Am), he introduced it through a field event or field materials. It is the same as when he rescued and forgave the woman caught in the scene of adultery, in which he proclaimed, "I am the light of the world" (John 8:12). Jesus's conversation shows that the site is both a workplace and a training ground. It means that the field is a good opportunity to share the gospel.

It makes it possible to convey God's intentions (words) through everyday encounters and conversations. Jesus also delivered the Word by transforming and applying it to actual life. It is like the question, "Do you want to get well?" (John 5:6), or to say, "A man who walks by day will not stumble, for he sees by this world's light. It is when he walks by night that he stumbles, for he has no light" (John 11:9). Here, no common biblical languages are used.

If the Word is compared to a code of law, the point of view is its interpretation and application. Don't we not mention the provisions of the code in everyday conversations? If only we have God's perspective, the language of everyday life, will be a field language. This field language naturally connects unbelief and faith. In other words, the field language means to make it suitable to the current situation based on the interpretation of God's perspective.

1. ONSITE MATERIAL

The work of the flesh is the basis for saving the spirit. Presenting God through field materials exerts great influence. Jesus approached the gospel as a matter of the flesh. Through the works of the flesh, he taught the works of the Holy Spirit. Knowing life, he fulfilled the needs of everyone he met. Jesus healed the sick, raised the dead, and gave fish and loaves to the hungry.

It is worth noting that Jesus made good use of the material in the field. Any material given to him was used as a valuable and most effective tool to preach the truth there. Jesus's conversations open our eyes to how we draw the spirit from the flesh. The things of the world (antitypes) are used as effective tools to explain heavenly things (types).

Its application is very direct, visual, and aural, allowing the listener and the viewer to understand accurately. Examples include light and salt, sunset and age discrimination, birds and worries, fox and evangelist life, barley bread and bread of life, vine and religious life, sheep and shepherd, wind and Spirit, day and night, work and rest, wine and banquet. All help explain principles such as death and resurrection, hunger and spirituality rich, the pain of childbirth and joy of birth, sin and slavery, and so on. All field materials were used as a medium for realizing important truths.

In the conversation with Nicodemus, the wind is used as the material: "The wind blows wherever it pleases. You hear its sound, but you cannot tell where it comes from or where it is going. So it is with everyone born of the Spirit" (John 3:8). He introduced the voluntariness of the Holy Spirit through the onsite material of wind. On that night, he used the wind blowing from the edge of the tent (wind is everywhere). Just as the wind blows randomly, so does the Holy Spirit.

If our world is under God's providence and rule, then nature and everyday affairs we face are good materials to show about God. The truth is hidden in them. Such materials are all around us if we look. One's entire life can be viewed through the prism of these field materials. It means that we may introduce the Word in any situation, event, or even in the small things. If these materials are utilized well, the message of God is transmitted easily and accurately.

I have another story. After graduating from high school, Young K. deeply wondered about his career path. He got drunk and went to the house of the evangelist of his church. As he was drunkenly talking about his worries, the preacher laid him on the sofa, where he fell asleep. After sleeping for a while, the young man woke up with a contrite heart and asked for a glass of water. The preacher asked his wife for two cups. She brought one cup that held clear water and another cup filled with dirty water. Putting the two cups of water on the table, the preacher asked the youth which water he would like to drink. The young man took the glass of clear water and drank it gleefully. The preacher then spoke to the young man, who had come to his senses. "Just as you chose clear water, God wants someone prepared with a clean heart."After this encounter, the young man corrected his way of thinking, entered the ministry, and became a pastor. He still can't forget what happened then and the evangelist who opened the way for him, holding him in the highest respect.

Jesus also pointed to Caesar's coin and asked, "whose image is this? And whose inscription?" (Mark 12:16).Using a coin, he preached the famous sermon, defeating the Jewish scheme of accusing with offerings: "Give back to Caesar what is Caesar's and to God what is God's" (Mark 12:17).In this scene, the visual effect is maximized.

A pastor offered a similar explanation using fifty dollars in cash. He crumpled the money and explained that its value did not change even if crumpled as long as the government guarantees its value. Likewise, even saved people make mistakes but are still valuable to God.

I once had a conversation about faith with Mr. C., who is in the computer business. He was fixing broken computers stacked to his left and right. When we talked about God, I explained to him that if you meet Jesus, you will know everything about him in the same way as you connect the power to the computer and immediately get all the information you need. In response, he nodded.

Once I was visiting an old friend. He told me that his wife had recently been to the emergency room several times with high blood pressure. I thought it would be good if I could go to their house and pray with them. On the way, I bought a small box of drinks and handed them over. His wife greeted me with joy, saying, "Just your visit is enough. You don't need to buy something."She attended a Catholic church, while my friend was not religious.

I tried using field materials and said to his wife, "I have prepared a better present for you, which I will give to you soon."She kept making a curious face until I sat on the sofa in a somewhat tense atmosphere. I said, "I want to pray for you, " breaking the awkward atmosphere.

Then she came to me with a bright smile and said, "Seems your prayer must be powerful. Thank you for praying for me." The three of us could then pray together in a light atmosphere. I had wanted to convey the gospel to my friend for a long time, but only then could I do it. However, if I hadn't used the onsite materials (a box of beverages), we would not have been able to pray together so easily.

2. ONSITE TEACHING

We say more than tens of thousands of words a day. However, if our conversations begin and end with the flesh, they will not be able to save the spirit. Jesus said, "The Spirit gives life; the flesh counts for nothing. The words I have spoken to you—they are full of Spirit and life" (John 6:63). It is not to say that the issue of eating and living is not important. Rather, it means that flesh is flesh and Spirit is Spirit. The places where our hearts and feet touch are in the field, and all the stories of our lives are within this field. So we can use it as a conversation that saves the spirit. But this depends on how we see the field and what perspectives we have.

For an easy example, if your child has suffered injustice at school or has stolen an item from the store, you should learn how to best use the occasion to teach about God. Depending on how you view the field, you can use it as an opportunity that saves the spirit. Life is a training ground for learning, teaching, listening, and speaking to try to engage in spiritual conversation. So it is a training ground for saving lives. Without this awareness, the important encounters and opportunities offered by the present will be lost.

The field can be the most effective time and place for

evangelism. Evangelism does not occur from afar. It's not just about reaching out to those who are far away. Rather, it's about all the encounters we face, from those involving our parents, siblings, relatives, friends, and neighbors to our fellow customers.

Jesus made good use of the situation in the field to enhance the faith of his disciples. And it seems that he maximized the transmission of meaning very effectively by using the surrounding circumstances well. We can find how wonderfully Jesus used it for the onsite teaching. These points are seen in many examples.

For example, at the end of the conversation with the Samaritan woman, the disciples set their hard-earned lunch before Jesus. The subject was food. When they said, "Rabbi, eat something" (John 4:31), he replied, "I have food to eat that you know nothing about" (John 4:32). They started to wonder, "Could someone have brought him food?" (John 4:33).

Jesus did not miss this chance and used it as an opportunity for the enlightenment of the truth. "My food is to do the will of him who sent me and to complete his work" (John 4:34).He taught them that the joy that the spiritual salvation of a person like this Samaritan woman brought was comparable to spiritual satiety; that is, God's food.

Onsite teaching continued. It was time for local Samaritans came to Jesus after hearing the Samaritan woman speak about him. It was a time when colored clothes were rare, and they must have been dressed in white or pale yellow, probably looking like rice waiting for harvest. He used this as material to teach evangelism to his disciples. "Don't you have a saying, 'It's still four months until harvest'?" (Introduction and interest). "I tell you, open your eyes and look at the fields! They are ripe for harvest" (transmission of the spiritual meaning; John 4:35). "Even now, the one who reaps draws a wage and harvests a crop for eternal life so that the sower and the reaper may be glad together" (quote scripture; John 4:36). "Thus, the saying, 'One sows and another reaps' is true. I sent you to reap what you have not worked for.

Others have done the hard work, and you have reaped the benefits of their labor" (convey meaning; John 4:35–38).

In the case of Philip, the site of the miracle of five loaves and two fishes became the most effective training ground. Jesus asked Philip to test him, knowing what he would do, saying, "Where shall we buy bread for these people to eat?" (John6:5).Jesus did not miss the chance and intentionally asked Philip to open his eyes. It is possible to speculate why he chose Philip and not the other disciples to test. Some claim it was because Philip was clever with calculations. Others say Philip was standing closer to Jesus and there was no need to add any special meaning.

However, we can infer from Philip's question in the fourth gospel. Near the end of his ministry, Philip receives a rebuke calling for a spiritual awakening while asking Jesus to show him God. "Don't you know me, Philip, even after I have been among you such a long time? Anyone who has seen me has seen the Father. How can you say, 'Show us the Father'" (John 14:9). Philip missed the image of God in Jesus. Philip's view was that something more needed to be opened.

The unprecedented and great miraculous opportunity of providing food for fifteen thousand men with five small barley loaves and two small fishes was also a special teaching site for Philip. It must have given his eyes a great opportunity to experience another perspective that transcended realistically impossible situations. He saw the disposition and power of God, who came as the Son of Man. It is what Jesus taught. Philip's confession is omitted, but I think Jesus took it as a good opportunity to open his perspective and not rule something as impossible according to his calculations. Jesus used the occasion where he made a great miracle, multiplied food, fed crowds, and eventually put Philip's quick calculation skills to shame. Philip's silence would tell his confession.

Jesus taught how to serve during the Last Supper of Passover in Mark's upper room on a day they journeyed far and covered the disciples' feet with dust. Jewish custom required a servant to wash their feet when guests arrived. It was then that the disciples looked at each other. Jesus got up from the table, took off his outer clothing, and wrapped a towel around his waist. After that, he poured water into a basin and began to wash his disciples' feet, drying them with the towel wrapped around him. Bewildered, the disciples found themselves in an awkward situation.

When it was Peter's turn, he couldn't stand it. "Lord, are you going to wash my feet? No, you shall never wash my feet" (John 13:6).

Jesus showed the example of humility and service, but he used it as an opportunity to teach the truth. "Those who have had a bath needs only to wash their feet; their whole body is clean. And you are clean, though not every one of you" (John 13:10).

The great truth comes so easily with onsite explanations. No one could get a better understanding than this. Those who believed in Jesus Christ and became children of God have already bathed, and there is no need to bathe again. Efforts to wash the dust off their feet, to repent of their daily sins and errors, are sufficient. Those who are unclean will wash their feet and still be dirty. But those who are clean will wash their feet ten times and still be clean. Judas Iscariot had not washed(John13: 1–11).[12]

The betrayal of Judas Iscariot was also taught by the parable of the vine and its branches. Judas's betrayal was vividly conveyed in the parable of the vine. The day after the Last Supper, and on that same night, Jesus prayed to God to preserve his disciples so that none would perish: "while I was with them, I protected them and kept them safe by that name you gave me. None has been lost except the one doomed to destruction so that Scripture would be fulfilled" (John17:12). During the supper, Judas Iscariot left to betray him.

After Jesus finished his high priestly prayer, he and the eleven

---

[12] William Hendriksen, *Gospel of John* (1959) Chapter 13, pp. 231–232.

remaining disciples left the city of Jerusalem. They moved across the Kidron Valley to the small garden of Gethsemane, where Jesus spent the night with them. Even though Jesus knew that Judas would come there to arrest him, he still went to that place. Jesus laid down his life for the sheep as a true shepherd would. Jesus knew better than anyone that the time to reveal his Father's glory was imminent. Knowing that a dark moment was close at hand, the burden on his heart must have been almost too heavy to bear. From the Kidron Valley to the garden, the vines in the vineyards were likened to Judas Iscariot, who betrayed and fell, leading to another educational site: "I am the vine, you are the branches. If you remain in me and I in you, you will bear much fruit; apart from me you can do nothing. If you do not remain in me, you are like a branch that is thrown away and withers; such branches are picked up, thrown into the fire and burned" (John15: 5–6).[13]

---

[13] William Hendriksen, *Gospel of John* (1959) See chapter 13, p. 233.

Chapter 5
TOOLS FOR EFFECTIVE CONVERSATIONS

DURING ANY ENCOUNTER AND CONVERSATION, MASTERED conversational skills allow one to communicate effectively. We need to acquire the skills that fit neighbors' needs and can reveal God in various ways at different situations. The following are some useful conversational tools that Jesus frequently used. If we adopt and use these tools well, it could help our conversations to be more clearer, give them authority, and make them linger in listeners' minds.

1. USE OF SYMMETRICAL LANGUAGE

In the words of Jesus, we can find that in many cases, words and sentences are used as substitutions, contrasts, and comparisons. Almost everywhere in the synoptic gospels we find this pattern of symmetry and contrast. For example, "I am telling you what I have seen in the Father's presence, and you do what you have heard from your father" (John 8:38). This contrast reflects the clear difference.("I and you, God the Father and the father of the flesh, what I have seen and what you have heard, I am telling and you do.") Jesus contrasts each phrase very delicately, making the accuracy of meaning possible through the clear transmission of words.

Symmetrical composition plays a role in revealing the meaning more clearly too. And at the same time, it adds authority to the words. This contrast is often used in drawing out the truth. For example, as seen in John 8, almost all of Jesus's words are expressed in the same way:

> Even if I testify on my own behalf, my testimony is valid, for I know where I came from and where I am going. But you have no idea where I come from or where I am going. You judge by human standards; I pass judgment on no one. But if I do judge, my decisions are true, because I am not alone. I stand with the Father, who sent me.(John 8:14–16) If you knew me, you would know my Father also.(John 8:19).I am going away, and you will look for me, and you will die in your sin. Where I go, you cannot come. (John 8:21) You are from below; I am from above. You are of this world; I am not of this world.(John 8:23)

The effects of symmetry and contrast limit the scope of the interpretation while providing clearer meaning to the already known facts. The first half, transposition, mainly shows facts or justifications. The second half gives explanations or claims. For example, in the expression, "Foxes have dens and birds have nests, but the Son of Man has no place to lay his head" (Matthew 8:20),it is explained that the hard life of Jesus is sufficiently reminiscent of the house of foxes and sparrows that we know. It has the effect of conveying meaning in an easy-to-understand manner through prior knowledge.

Likewise, almost all sayings and aphorisms are expressed in these symmetrical forms:"When evening comes, you say, 'It will be fair weather, for the sky is red,' and in the morning, 'Today it will be stormy, for the sky is red and overcast.' You know how to interpret the appearance of the sky, but you cannot interpret the signs of the times" (Matthew16:2–3).

By making good use of these verses in our daily expressions, we can help the other party to understand more clearly and adding authority to our words.

2. ANALOGY

Parables are used to lead listeners to understanding the heavenly things. It is not just a story that moves and impresses. It becomes the force that guides our spiritual life; in the synoptic gospels, there are at least fifteen parables featuring Jesus speaking. The easiest way to understand the indescribable reality of heaven is to make people learn indirectly through facts and stories that one can realistically accept. The Bible says that Jesus taught using parables, "so that, 'they may be ever seeing but never perceiving, and ever hearing but never understanding; otherwise they might turn and be forgiven!'"(Mark4:12). Since things in the flesh speak of things that are of the Spirit, the parable will establish itself as a story as long as one does not attain enlightenment. However, those who receive the Spirit of God by seeing the reality in the pattern have confidence and receive more knowledge about the kingdom of God.

In general, if the story aims to give empathy and lessons by grasping the main flow of the whole story, the parable of Jesus deals with each verse or word with great precision down to the finest of details. Even if it is a metaphor or a simile, it contains the truth. Famous parables of the lost son, the sower, the parable of the sheep and the shepherd, and so on, contain deep impressions and important details of getting to know God.

The parable of the vine and the branches is given the same meaning: "who eats my blood and my flesh." It teaches very close communication relationships. Just as a branch dies when broken or falls from a tree must be nourished to bear fruit, one needs to live for Jesus Christ as Jesus lives for God. In other words, life in a relationship with Jesus is he in me and I in him. Salvation lies in the confession that Jesus is Lord and in the unity of life through Jesus Christ. The definition of faith taught by Jesus is living in a relationship of oneness within Jesus and being supplied with life.

3. SUBJUNCTIVE FORM

The subjunctive form is one of the methods Jesus effectively used to open spiritual vision. This form is mainly used in conversation topics to overcome negative situations in the present with positive views. It is also used to convince people about what will happen. The effect of this subjunctive is to add possibility to the claim and persuade others to open their eyes more:"then what if you see the Son of Man ascend to where he was before!" (John 6:62).

The subjunctive itself is used to convey the truth and enlighten listeners. When the Jews demanded proof, asking, "where is your father?" Jesus answered with a subjunctive:"You do not know me or my Father, If you knew me, you would know my Father also" (John 8:19).

The subjunctive can also be seen as a way to move forward in uncomfortable conversations. For example, to the embarrassing question of a Samaritan woman, "You are a Jew, and I am a Samaritan woman. How can you ask me for a drink [for Jews do not associate with Samaritans](John4:9).

The subjunctive not only opens the way out of the Samaritan woman's embarrassing question but also brings a leading position:

"If you knew the gift of God and who it is that asks you for a drink, you would have asked him, and he would have given you living water" (John 4:10). How wonderful a breakthrough and leading conversation it is!

I have a personal anecdote that relates to this topic. Unbelieving friend K complained that a church not too far from his house was making life difficult in his neighborhood. "It's noisy every evening, my house value continues to go down, and cars cover the whole residential area, especially on Sundays. I will not leave this church alone."

"Yeah," I replied. "As you said, this church did not consider your disadvantage. But you also do not know God at all. If you had known God, you would have already enrolled in that church." Despite the strained atmosphere, I delivered God's message aggressively in the defense.

4. IMPLICIT EXPRESSIONS

Verbs

Jesus's conversations are expressed concisely. His authority and ability to see man quench his spiritual thirst as an omniscient person stand out. In the one-on-one conversations shown in the synoptic gospels, it is found that the present-tense verbs are mostly used in a very direct and concise imperative form. These expressions also show authority. "Follow me" (John 1:43), "Fill the jars with water" (John 2:7), "Now draw some out and take it to the master of the banquet" (John 2:8), "Go, call your husband and come back" (John 4:16), "Get up! Pick up your mat and walk" (John 5:8), "It is I; don't be afraid" (John 6:21), "Take off the grave clothes and let him go" (John 11:44), "Here is your mother" (John 19:27), and so on. Approaching the essence of the problem and giving a solution reveal his authority.

Titles

At the wedding feast in Cana, Jesus reminded Mary, his mother, of his messianic works, even with a simple title. When Mary saw that the wine was running out, she quietly went to Jesus and said, "They have no more wine" (John 2:3). There was no need for elaborate explanations in the conversation between mother and son. She remembered how Jesus was born. She had seen the beginning of his ministry with his six disciples.

However, Mary, who still did not fully understand the public messianic ministry, needed to be reminded with the following words:"Woman, why do you involve me? My hour has not yet come" (John2:4).

He said the word "woman" to help her know that the plan and the time are separate from God's point of view. Apart from the earthly things and his work was precisely on God's eternal salvation plan within an intimate relationship with God. The word "woman" is used to make her recognize him as the spiritual Messiah, not the son of the flesh. The expression helps to secure such a perspective. "Woman" is used as an honorific title here. However, it pointed out that he objectified his mother.

The gospel of Matthew emphasizes securing this perspective. Another scene also appears when Jesus spoke to the crowd. Mary and Jesus's brothers stood outside, wanting to see. Then Jesus stretched out his hand and taught his disciples by asking, "Who is my mother, and who are my brothers?" Pointing to his disciples, he answered, "Here are my mother and my brothers. For whoever does the will of my Father in heaven is my brother and sister and mother" (Matthew 12:48–50). These words mean that the kingdom of God is not of the flesh but the spirit, and he urged not only the disciples but also Mary and his brothers to secure that spiritual perspective.

The consideration of Jesus Christ is truly deep. This word, planted in Mary, can be seen as an implicit expression to make her realize it at some point. This title of "woman," used at the first miracle in Cana, was heard again by Mary at the scene of the great suffering on the last crucifixion: "woman, here is your son" (John 19:27). I think we can find the answer to using this title here. If Mary only looked at Jesus as a son, her heart would have carried the pain of the crucifixion suffered by that physical son until the day she died. But if she looked to Jesus as the Messiah who saved the world, she would see God's infinite love, even in the suffering. It became possible to draw attention again to God's grace for what was given to her. A single title is what saved her. And it means that the title given to Mary is more meaningful than the fact that Jesus entrusted his mother to his disciple John.

Silence

How would you react if your boss suddenly asked to meet you in a few days? You might be curious and wonder if you had done something wrong. Reflecting on the possibilities, there would likely be some tension and caution too. The dialogues and reactions in the Gospels lead us to think that Jesus used silence a lot. It is shown that there were many elements of silence in his words, for example, "Do you want to get well?" (John 5:6), and, "Who do people say the Son of Man is?" (Matthew 16:13).

Silence allows us to look inward and replaces numerous explanations. For example, scared by the accusations of the Jews, Pilate asked Jesus, "What is truth?" (John 18:38).Jesus remained silent. Excuses or defenses do not help at all. But silence makes him listen to his conscience's voice, and he will judge by himself.

At the Last Supper, when Jesus spoke about betrayal among one of the disciples, the disciples looked at each other in fear: "Lord, who is it?" (John 13:25). The brief silence was also the last opportunity to urge Judas Iscariot to repent.

Even the talkative Samaritan woman was told to "Go, call your husband and come back" (John 4:15), which made her look at herself in silence. Silence turns us inward, letting us hear the inner voice.

Silence sometimes has great effects. In the case of a woman caught in adultery, the effect of such silence is well demonstrated. Jesus said to a group gathered around him, "Let any of you who is without sin be first to throw a stone at her" (John8:7).He then bent down and wrote on the ground using his finger. He let a long period of silence transpire to calm their emotions and allow them to hear their inner voices.

Prophecy and Encouragement

In keeping with the plan of salvation of the Father, from a foresight standpoint, Jesus foretold events progressively or continuously according to the faith and needs of the disciples. We can see that he told his disciples several times about the fears and hardships they would face so that they could cultivate the strength necessary to endure that fear and hardship: "You do not realize now what I am doing, but later you will understand" (John 13:7). "A woman giving birth to a child has pain because her time has come; but when her baby is born she forgets the anguish because of her joy that a child is born into the world. So with you: Now is your time of grief, but I will see you again, and you will rejoice, and no one will take away your joy" (John16: 21–22).

As the execution drew near, Jesus comforted his disciples by balancing the hardships and fears they would soon face with the great joy of his pending Resurrection and the promise of the Holy Spirit to come. He described, "It was just before the Passover Festival. Jesus knew that the time had come for him to leave this world and go to the Father. Having loved his own who were in the world, he loved them to the end" (John 13:1).

Disciples, after realizing Jesus's words were part of the process of fulfilling God's eternal salvation plan, could have been strengthened to stand firm in promise and trust in confidence.

Chapter 6
CONFLICT AND COPING

PEOPLE OFTEN ASSOCIATE JESUS WITH AN IDYLLIC ATMOSPHERE, like a painting of him with a staff in one hand and a sheep in the other. or the image of him as a calm figure teaching people while sitting or giving a sermon on the mount. However, it is not an exaggeration to say that Jesus's life saw much trouble and strife. For three and a half years, his public life was that of persuasion and struggle with claims and arguments against the Jews' calls for evidence. When he claimed that he was the Son of God, accusations of blasphemy poured in, and critics demanded evidence of his work. The Jews were represented by religious leaders who mobilized theological, theoretical, and sometimes even physical force to destroy his claims. It made religious leaders cling to the foundation of their survival. None can approach it more thoroughly than that. Jesus was a target, and wherever he went, he was threatened with losing his life.

Therefore, the plan to complete the preaching of the gospel during a crisis would not have been possible without being well prepared. Sometimes we say that we are doing God's work under the banner of faith, but it is quite different from a reckless and haphazard approach. On the last cross, the expression, "It is finished," implies that Jesus paid the penalty of death for the salvation of humankind. Yet, it also tells us that the entire plan for the evangel has been accomplished.

Suppose the temple-cleansing incident was the first official act to show his appearance to Jewish religious leaders. News of the incident must have then spread rapidly among Jews. Also, through the healing of the blind man on the Sabbath, which was imperatively forbidden, Jesus made the extraordinary remark that he is the Son of God and the Lord of the Sabbath. It caused serious repercussion not only among Jewish religious leaders but also in Jewish masses. By building a symmetrical force, Jesus was able to highlight himself in a short time. It can be imagined as part of a strategy to fight an organization with a large Jewish religious leaders' group. In particular, the large crowds gathered at the miracle site made it impossible to ignore his power and influence. Some view the six-month evangelistic trip—including border visits to Tire and Sidon, and the Decapolis and Malmanuta, and the vast northern regions—the so-called Galilean missionary as a strategy for entering Jerusalem.

Suppose Jesus were to fight alone against the great organization called the Sanhedrin. It could be seen as part of the evangelism strategy for the Galilean ministry to start in the north and enter Jerusalem through the center. Jesus rode a donkey into Jerusalem, and all the people came to meet him carrying palm branches. The wave of welcome was so great that it covered all Jerusalem. It was too great a force against religious leaders.

Jesus knew exactly the time of completion of the gospel ministry. Contrary to what the disciples thought, when his fame reached its peak and even foreigners, some Greek, came to him, Jesus said that the hour of his death on the cross and the time to glorify Father and complete his work was imminent(John 12:23–28). Before entering Jerusalem, he taught his disciples how to deal with the dangers they would face in the end, which shows how well he had prepared.

When Jesus went to Jerusalem for the Feast of Tabernacles, his plan was revealed. Considering the circumstances, it was very dangerous to participate in the festival held in the temple of Jerusalem. The Jews wanted to arrest and kill him as all Israelites should attend the temple. Furthermore, he should have to proclaim the truth under this high-risk circumstance. He ascended secretly in the middle of the festival, three days later. As it was still a time when pilgrims were trying to participate in the festival, he went up secretly, even escaping the latecomers. It is unknown whether Jesus used the main road during off-hours (night or dawn), side roads, or other roads that were not often used.

Throughout, Jesus's actions were intentional and precise. Even though his brothers had urged him to go to the temple three days earlier, Jesus deliberately delayed the time of his departure. He went to the Jerusalem temple and did not reveal himself until the middle of the Feast of the Tabernacle, when he suddenly appeared in the temple. Jesus's late appearance divided people's opinions about his identity and made them either welcome him or be uncooperative. But eventually, he gained their support.

When Jesus appeared, he drew the attention of a waiting crowd. As he began preaching, hostile forces failed to arrest him publicly because numerous pilgrims attended, and the crowds who knew him as a prophet used fencing as a shield against the threat. The Jews who were determined to kill him were baffled.[14]

It is astonishing that Jesus, for the most part, preached the word amid strife but was still able to clearly reveal the truth. The following review of the content or development of the dialogue shows this did not happen by chance. It was well planned and intentional.

It is different from improvised and emotionally driven conversations. In other words, he was able to take enough information in advance and approach it with a plan. Despite

---

[14] William Hendriksen, *Gospel of John* (1959) See chapter 7, pp. 5–8.

emotional situations, approaching dialectically and logically allowed him to achieve his intended purpose.

The following shows an introduction to the situation of the conflicts and the contents of the conversations in different situations.

CONFLICT CASE 1

Chapters 7 and 8 of the gospel of John introduce the situation of the conflicts. Here, we'll see how to deal with the conflicting events during the Feast of Tabernacles (John 7).

> Not until halfway through the Feast did Jesus go up to the temple courts and begin to teach. The Jews there were amazed and asked, "How did this man get such learning without having been taught?" Jesus answered, "My teaching is not my own. It comes from the one who sent me. Anyone who chooses to do will of God will find out whether my teaching comes from God or whether I speak on my own. Whoever speaks on his own does so to gain personal glory, but he who seeks the glory of the one who sent him is a man of truth; there is nothing false about him.

> "Has not Moses given you the law? Yet not one of you keeps the law. Why are you trying to kill me?""You are demon-possessed," the crowd answered."Who is trying to kill you?" Jesus said to them, "I did one miracle, and you are all amazed.

> "Yet, because Moses gave you circumcision (though actually, it did not come from Moses,

the patriarchs), you circumcise a boy on the Sabbath. Now, if a boy can be circumcised on the Sabbath so that the law of Moses may not be broken, why are you angry with me for healing a man's whole body on the Sabbath? Stop judging by mere appearances, but instead judge correctly."
(John 7:14–24)

Jesus's teaching was amazing. The Jews had to admit his excellency. Nevertheless, their intentions and public opinion were to bring him down and kill him. Criticism of academic background and origin is presented as an objective basis that can undermine his teaching. Here, it is interesting to see how Jesus leads in the part related to academic discipline. In the dialogue, answers are given precisely in line with the context of the Jews' accusations, and Jesus's excellent communication skills are revealed, also revealing God's perspective and message.

The reaction of the Jews reflects their prior position: "How did this man get such learning without having been taught?" (John7:15).The position of the Jews is evident. It is an expression that he did not learn the scripture nor its interpretation at the rabbinic school. If we say in today's language that because he didn't major in theology, and didn't have any qualifications, so his teaching was wrong. As a result, his words have negative connotations and demeaned as unworthy to hear. Therefore, whatever he said must be wrong! The implication was that Jesus was uttering his personal opinions about religious matters.[15]

These evaluations of their view repeatedly appear in other places as well. It was probably their hidden intentional public opinion to undermine Jesus's outstanding teachings. It triggered the dispute as they demanded objective proof based on academic background. Hence, they completely missed the possibility that

---

[15] William Hendriksen, *Gospel of John* (1959) Chapter 7, p. 10.

Jesus's words were being delivered from a higher place than any Jewish education courses. Jesus's answer fits precisely within the context of the Jews' accusations. Jesus said, "My teaching is not my own. It comes from the one who sent me" (John 7:16).In other words, what he was teaching was not his own opinion but came from God. It is a completely new perspective, not what he learned on his own. Furthermore, according to his claim, it even implied that to reject him was to reject the one who sent him. Jesus is disproving logic: "Anyone who chooses to do the will of God will find out whether my teaching comes from God or whether I speak on my own" (John 7:17). Could a prophet who came on his own do what Jesus did? Could he reveal the glory of the one who sent him? He who speaks his own words will not be able to do so. This statement makes us aware of two facts at the same time. The leaders are ridiculed because the origin is completely different, and the authority to hear directly from the Father is a transcendent privilege that cannot be countered by anything or anyone else. Its origin is absolute superior authority, not a subject of comparison.

Now, Jesus, who seemed to be on the defensive, turned to the offensive: "Has not Moses given you the law? Yet not one of you keeps the law. Why are you trying to kill me?"(John 7:19).It was a question that pierced their cores.

Their hypocrisy was exposed, and the dispute heated up. In general, the way to settle disputes is to calm down when triggered. However, Jesus aggravated it, and they strongly resisted. But Jesus was intentionally leading them to a greater truth. The crowd answered, "You are demon-possessed. Who is trying to kill you?" (John 7:20). Their hypocritical views that led them to accuse Jesus of being possessed by a demon were exposed. The terms used in the conflict reveal the Jewish leaders' primary colors.

A sudden stabbing in the core will make one panic and pretend to speak the truth. The religious leaders sat in Moses' seat and were treated with respect, and they called themselves Moses' disciples. Adorned with all righteous and godly aspects, the usual form of insisting on holiness and justice was invisible amid conflict, and the things inside intentions were exposed. Then six months later, religious leaders led Jesus Christ to be crucified out of jealousy. They were more concerned with their glory and benefit.[16]

In a conflict, it's not easy to catch the other side's point of view. The point of view of the so-called religious leaders, collectively known as the high priests and Pharisees, missed everything except what was seen by their own eyes. They keep their positions as they said, "You do not realize that it is better for you that one man dies for the people than that the whole nation perish" (John11:50). Their views were limited only to their own, and they completely missed Jesus's and God's views. When one is limited to his outlook, he will lose the perspectives of others and cling to self-interests.

Controversy ignores even the procedure of Moses' Law, which they had always guarded. There was no change in their egocentric views of the benefit of self or group in their hearts. They used the blameless Son of God as a sacrificial lamb for their benefit. And they further mobilized their minions to find and kill him.

They ignored that they serve God under the premise of their safety and benefit. The Mosaic Torah they received is a law of love, but they didn't mind making it a convenient law of hate and death. Although it was right for Jesus to make people whole on the Sabbath by obeying the Law of Moses, they tried to kill him, and their anger showed how absurd they were.

To open their confined field of vision, Jesus touched on the Word of God. Using God's Word of truth as the yardstick reveals how far they had gone astray: "Stop judging by mere appearances but instead judge correctly"(John 7:24). Judgment of disputes requires fair enforcement of laws and procedures to reveal how

---

[16] William Hendriksen, *Gospel of John* (1959) See chapter 7, pp. 9–14.

untrue claims are. In a conflict where consensus is rare, truth is the only touchstone of judgment. It will prove itself true someday.

CONFLICT CASE 2

Even as he spoke, many put their faith in him. To the Jews who had believed him, Jesus said, "If you hold to my teaching, you are really my disciples. Then you will know the truth, and the truth will set you free." They answered him, "We are Abraham's descendants and have never been slaves of anyone. How can you say that we shall be set free?" Jesus replied, "Very truly I tell you, everyone who sins is a slave to sin. Now a slave has no permanent place in the family, but a son belongs to it forever. So if the Son sets you free, you will be free indeed. I know that you are Abraham's descendants. Yet you are ready to kill me, because you have no room for my word. I am telling you what I have seen in the Father's presence, and you do what you have heard from your father." "Abraham is our father," they answered. "If you were Abraham's children," said Jesus, "then you would do what Abraham did. As it is, you are looking for a way to kill me, a man who has told you the truth that I heard from God. Abraham did not do such things. You are doing the works of your own father." "We are not illegitimate children," they protested. "The only Father we have is God himself." Jesus said to them, "If God were your Father, you would love me, for I came from God. I have not come on my own; God sent me. Why is my language not clear to you? Because you are unable to hear what

I say. You belong to your Father, the devil, and you want to carry out your father's desire. He was a murderer from the beginning, not holding to the truth, for there is no truth in him. When he lies, he speaks his native language, for he is a liar and the father of lies. Yet because I tell the truth, you do not believe me! Can any of you prove me guilty of sin? If I am telling the truth, why don't you believe me? whoever belongs to God hears what God says. The reason you do not hear is that you do not belong to God." The Jews answered him,"Aren't we right in saying that you are a Samaritan and demon-possessed?""I am not possessed by a demon," said Jesus,"but I honor my Father and you dishonor me. I am not seeking glory for myself; but there is one who seeks it, and he is the judge. Very truly I tell you whoever obeys my word will never see death." At this the Jews exclaimed,"Now we know that you are demon-possessed! Abraham died and so did the prophets, yet you say that whoever obeys your word will never taste death. Are you greater than our father Abraham? He died, and so did the prophets. Who do you think you are?" Jesus replied,"If I glorify myself, my glory means nothing. My Father, whom you claim as your God, is the one who glorifies me. Though you do not know him, I know him. If I said I did not, I would be a liar like you, but I do know him and obey his word. Your father Abraham rejoiced at the thought of seeing my day; he saw it and was glad.""You are not yet fifty years old,"they said to him,"and you have seen Abraham!""Very truly I tell you," Jesus answered,"before Abraham was born, I am!"

> At this, they picked up stones to stone him, but
> Jesus hid himself, slipping away from the temple
> grounds. (John 8:30–59)

This text is also a good example of the development process of conflict in a harsh atmosphere. We see Jesus exposing their plot to kill with hostility even though there is no evil or defect in Jesus, the Son of God, who was called and obeyed, heals the sick, and reveals the glory of God. The text unfolds the way Jesus reveals the truth amid the fierce debate during the Feast of Tabernacles.

Jesus knew the position of the Jews and revealed his identity in line with their arguments. He also gave a harsh rebuke to the Jewish leaders who self-proclaimed themselves as Moses' disciples yet practiced hypocrisy. Jesus said that they were not descendants of Abraham but slaves of sin and descendants of the devil because they did not accept the rebuke and showed strong resistance, foreshadowing that the situation would end violently.

Conflict is an internal reaction, whereas an assault is a physical, mental, and external shock caused by external threats, a sense of crisis, or conspiracy. And when it comes to conflict, situations usually follow a certain cycle.

It is referred to as the circular curve of conflict. Each individual's values, culture, background, circumstances, and so on are ignited if they collide with those of others at some point(trigger).It becomes an ignition point, leading to a rise in emotions and suddenly erupts into violence.

First, they show passive resistance in a cooperative atmosphere. Then they openly assert themselves, which leads to a bold, firm state. A characteristic feature of these stages is that the most important emotions are presented clearly in primary colors. When each party begins to have violent reactions to each other, they focus their gazes on one place and raise their voices in one direction; things other than that focus are excluded. However, each still listen and respond to what the other person says.

This firm state then accelerates to a critical point. Eventually, it turns into an explosive state of ignoring the person or the person's words, which leads to threatening and violent behavior. At this point, one pushes his argument without listening to the other person and a rational response is no longer expected. Whether a tactical withdrawal is necessary should be considered at this moment. After that, there is a decelerating period, and the rational state is restored. The emotional reaction is calmed and a normal appearance regained.

The behavior of the Jews clearly shows the same shape as the circular curve of conflict. When Jesus exposed their conspiracy to kill, the situation turned for the worse, and the Jews began to express their views adamantly. Although Jesus gave heavy and harsh rebukes according to the situation's progress, they also accused Jesus of being half Samaritan, accelerating the situation. Furthermore, they added to the previously mentioned words, "whoever obeys my word, will never see death" (John 8:51), and affirmed he was demon-possessed. Afterward, when Jesus said, "Your father Abraham rejoiced at the thought of seeing my day; he saw it and was glad" (John 8:56). The conflict, despite the sarcasm, suddenly reached the critical point when Jesus said, "before Abraham was born, I am!" (John 8:58), in response to their arguments of, "how can you say 'I was before Abraham' while you are not even fifty years old?" (John 8:57).

When the Jews entered firm state where they no longer heard, the situation escalated and went beyond rational thinking, quickly leading to a state of violence (critical point)with their attempts to stone Jesus to death. Then Jesus hid and escaped.

Conflict management is mainly taught as to police and security personnel. It teaches the importance of focusing on a given situation, removing other factors, and not expanding the scope of the problem. It also teaches the importance of respecting the individual and preventing the person from saying or doing anything that may provoke an argument. In many cases, the method of conveying the conversation, not the content, can escalate the situation and lead to further dispute. Instead, conflict management, teaches the person to express his clear position and attitude and explains the disadvantages that would arise if the argument and situation worsens. It suggests alternatives, decisions that need to be made, and gives people instructions to avoid being disadvantaged and getting into trouble. However, if someone does not respond and shows resistance, the authorized person will forcibly suppress.

Even though it is common knowledge to try to calm a conflict at the earliest possible stage (trigger) to prevent it from reaching a violent situation, Jesus accelerated the conflict by exposing it: "Yet not one of you keeps the law. Why are you trying to kill me?" (John 7:19). He, who had seemed to be defensive, went on offense.

It seems that he intended to convey the greater truth by exposing their hypocrisy with a question that got to the heart of the matter. In a harsh rebuke to the Jewish leaders, who claimed to be the descendants of Abraham and disciples of Moses, and who harbored the desire to kill him, Jesus told them that it was they who did not obey the Law and who committed hypocrisy. He said that they were not descendants of Abraham but servants of sin and descendants of the devil.

The rebuke is intense: "You belong to your father, the devil, and you want to carry out your father's desire. He was a murderer from the beginning, not holding to the truth, for there is no truth in him. When he lies, he speaks his native language, for he is a liar and the father of lies" (John 8:44).The severe rebuke revealed the essential corruption of life at its core.

Jesus pointed out that the fundamental reason for not hearing the Word lies in the hidden sinfulness. There was no trace of God's love in them. Eventually, he claimed they did not belong to God: "The reason you do not hear is that you do not belong to God" (June 8:47).

Jesus focused on the issue of their words, "Abraham is our

father," and revealed valuable truths from there. However, the Jews' attitude toward this claim did not change but was slandered once again, insisting on their legitimacy and arrogantly stating that they are Jews, but you are of Samaritan and demon-possessed? What they really meant was this, "We were not born of fornication, but you were!"

Jesus responded, "I am not possessed by a demon, but I honor my Father and you dishonor me. I am not seeking glory for myself; but there is one who seeks it, and he is the judge" (John 8:50). The enraged Jews no longer listened to him. And once a direction is set, it inevitably leads to a predictable outcome. This was no exception. They drove him away.

Despite repeatedly rebuking them, the firm state of the Jews escalated violently, going beyond rational thinking and into a state of violence. Nevertheless, Jesus gave them an invitation: "Very truly I tell you whoever obeys my word will never see death" (John 8:15).

If the Jewish people used violence to settle disputes, Jesus was using truth as his main weapon. It is also evident that Jesus was accurately looking at the Jews' point of view and was logically extending their points of view: "Though you do not know him, I know him. If I said I did not, I would be a liar like you, but I do know him and obey his word"(John 8:55).Meanwhile, the eyes of the hostile Jewish religious leaders focused on the speaker's mouth, aiming at and searching for the decisive clue that would bring him down.

During a dispute, one need to keep in mind what he claim and what he gain as that is more important than the conflict itself. To do that, one need to know what actions to take, how to use his communication skills to his fullest, and what alternatives are necessary as the situation progresses.

Ironically, the emotional shift amplified during conflict clearly expresses what the problem is. It also accurately exposes the inner intentions in return. In the raging conflict involving Jesus, there were great truths proclaimed amid the protests. Namely, that Jesus is the Son of God and has existed for eternity: "So if the Son sets you free, you will be free indeed" (John 8:36), "If God were your Father, you would love me, for I came from God. I have not come on my own; God sent me" (John 8:42), "Very truly I tell you, whoever obeys my word will never see death" (June 8:51), "If I glorify myself, my glory means nothing. My Father, whom you claim as your God, is the one who glorifies me" (June 8:54), and "before Abraham was born, I am!" (June 8:58).The truth has already been proclaimed, and the truth itself will work.

Jesus's tactical withdrawal seems to have been preplanned from the start. As the crowd was about to pick up stones, Jesus hid and escaped from the temple. We can imagine that Jesus entered the site with an exit already in place because the thought that the situation could become rough and threatening was likely very much on his mind.

Examples of this tactical withdrawal are also found elsewhere. The fourth evangelist often expressed the ways of avoiding these crises from God's point of view, "Because his hour had not yet come" (John 7:30).When John the Baptist was beheaded and a religious threat approached, Jesus left Judea and fled to Galilee. He also escaped under various circumstances similar to this, which testifies to Jesus's strategic withdrawal plan. Even in the gospel of Matthew, when giving the disciples an evangelistic tour, Jesus taught, "When you are persecuted in one place, flee to another" (Matthew 10:23).

During his ministry, whenever a crisis moment approached, Jesus hid and waited. Similarly, he waited for three days before suddenly appeared at the Feast of Tabernacles. He first let the audience form a defensive wall against Jews who wanted to arrest him, thereby neutralizing their arrest strategy.

Conversations do not always take place in a cordial and cooperative atmosphere. Sometimes conversations are peppered with sarcasm, arrogance, jealousy, disrespectfulness, and derogatory remarks. And so, with intimidation, violence is often inevitable. This phenomenon is common in our surroundings.

Conflicts range from political demands to external coercion in restraining the beliefs of groups or individuals. Marriages to unbelievers or religious persecution by family members also cause much friction. It is also common in many other religions or pseudo-groups.

They also appear among church members. It appears explicitly in places where religious interests, money, honor, and issues of the opposite sex are related. Unfortunately, conflicts within churches of the same denomination sometimes escalate into legal issues. The mental, physical, material, and religious damages suffered by those involved are considerable. Such conflicts and similar situations occur so frequently that anyone who has regularly attended a church, no matter how big or small, has encountered them directly or indirectly.

Without knowing how to deal with conflicts, one cannot overcome them and will fall into a defenseless situation. If left to accelerate, the conflict will amplify out of control. A vague fear of conflict, a lack of spiritual courage, or a lack of appropriate countermeasures can lead to a situation deteriorating beyond its control.

It is necessary to recognize and prioritize the conflict's factors to overcome those that cause serious obstacles. A good observation considers what risks these situations pose, what the consequences will be if they continue, and how often these situations are likely to occur.

These observations aid early resolution of the problem after efforts have been made to find out its root cause. If the cause is accurately identified, one can find a clue to a solution. It is necessary to make a list to do this. Think about the dangers of those problems, and seek and work on positive ways to overcome them. If these issues are not addressed early, the situation will become more difficult as it progresses.

The first thing to deal with in a conflict is to check whether you are in a position to control the given situation. This discernment allows you to decide whether to approach now, wait for help, or take a tactical withdrawal. This principle applies equally to matters large or small and whether in complex conflict situations or just in our daily encounters. The defenseless and unchecked approach easily breaks down one's defense wall.

The most important thing to consider in a conflict or assault situation is the person's nature and the site. It is important to know who the target audience is. Gather and deal with relevant information whenever possible. It must also consider the person's emotional state, special circumstances (illness or unusual reaction), or other characteristics. It would help if you also considered where the location is, whether there are people around or with them, whether the atmosphere is harsh or conducive to conversation or cooperation, and whether conversations may be interrupted by the surroundings.

Here are three ways to deal with a situation over which you have control:

1. Remove the impeding factors.
2. Isolate it if you cannot remove it.
3. If you can't contain a factor, try to minimize its impact.

Minimization means changing the environment, making the next best choice, allocating the time to another program, or trying to find another way. Being indifferent is the last option if you want to protect yourself.

If you decide that the situation is out of your control, there may be no need to step in. Avoiding the position, tactical withdrawal is the right response. If you feel that you cannot control the situation, you may need to seek help or devise other measures to get the situation under your control. You may be able to obtain knowledge by seeking cooperation from others or through guidance books, social networks, or lectures. It may also be helpful to have a spiritual leader or mentor close by who can offer you faith-based counsel. As Christians, the usual communication channels within church membership can help a lot.

And if circumstances deem it appropriate, it may also be necessary to take legal protection from police and other public authorities to protect your safety. Under certain circumstances, you may need to protect yourself and others. It is best not to involve yourself with a person or situation that is difficult for you to handle.

Reconciliation, forgiveness, and praying for the help of the Holy Spirit are weapons a Christian can measure. But above all else, your efforts to maintain your faith and preserve it from evil should come first.

A Christian's surest way is to respond to the Word and stand tall. The Word is the last stronghold of the believers. Least of all, even if the situation is difficult to control, we should try to maintain an attitude that shows the glory of God by standing in the truth.

The world collapsed because Jesus stood in the truth. A Christian's clear way is to stand to the Word. He glorifies and takes glory:"Be still, and know that I am God; I will be exalted among the nations, I will be exalted in the earth" (Psalm 46:10).

CONCLUSION

Jesus has lived the same days that are given to us. But he was always in God and showed a conversation that revealed God. Jesus's conversation shows that when man meets God, a radical change occurs. Our Christian lives should try to emulate and be inspired by Jesus in our everyday encounters and conversations.

Both the unbeliever and the believer are under the general grace of God. In fact, we are all objects of God's grace. Even unbelievers do their best to protect their families from the basic standpoint of security for their well-being. Sincerity, sweat, and tears are things we all share. Everyone is trying to find happiness, satisfaction, and loyalty to their own. God hates sin. But man is always the object of his love, and there is no difference in grade. So eternal life is promised to everyone who believes in Jesus Christ.

If God is the foundation of life, then loving our neighbors is what pleases him. We Christians should be able to reach out to them as we were once unbelievers too. Loving our neighbors is life itself, and the value of one's existence lies in the images of each other drawn in the minds of neighbors. That is the reality of my existence.

The future is sealed, and we cannot know who is destined to be saved. It is up to God's wisdom. Our position is that we must preach the gospel to everyone, which will reveal God's glory.

We could convey the Word in today's encounters and conversations. Attempting "Jesus conversations" will be beneficial for others and me in its spiritual development. Even the briefest everyday encounters could lead to a real interest in our lives. Jesus's conversations make us look first at the work of God. It contrasts with our inner-centered feelings, selfish desires, and hearts that seek profit or glory. What does God want? What does he want to say? These questions expand our spiritual horizons and enhance our abilities to see others on a deeper level.

But how can we continue to live in the glory of God and for our neighbors?

Awareness of the presence of the Holy Spirit makes it possible to have constant and intimate communion with him. We can constantly ask and rely on the help of the Holy Spirit. This understanding and way of life give us a way to fulfill the long-standing aspirations of all Christians.

We need to get into the habit of looking back at the conversations that have taken place and ask ourselves the following:

1. Have I approached them from God's perspective?
2. Was I aware of the other person's point of view?
3. Did I say yes or no?
4. Have I tried marshal?

After reflecting, we could take it further: "What else could I have delivered?""It would have been better if I told him that way!" "Was it the best way to deal with the situation?"and so on. We can use previous analyses as a foundation to try again. These efforts will also be able to enhance our conversational proficiencies. With more and more encounters, you will develop various coping skills and become better able to perceive the souls of your neighbors.

If we are in the conversation of Jesus, we could say that we are in God's presence and always doing what pleases him!

As we try to have a conversation to reach out to our neighbors' needs and convey the Word of God, I expect it will bring benefits, small or large, and result in positive changes to our lives. We should look forward to taking advantage of the precious moments provided by encounters and expect to see further growth in our conversational styles, depths of content, and the hope that the conversation of Jesus will bring us closer to the needs of our neighbors. In being able to lead the conversation in faith, we can look forward to seeing the power of the Word of God and change in others—all in the presence of the Holy Spirit, who will help us to move one step further to a lives that reveal the glory of God.

Appendix:

FOLLOWING JESUS'S FOUR-STEP DIALOGUE EVANGELISM

Following are additional conversations using Jesus's four-step dialogue evangelism with marshal.

1. CONVERSATION WITH THE SAMARITAN WOMAN

So he came to a town in Samaria called Sychar, near the plot of ground Jacob had given to his son Joseph.

Jacob's well was there, and Jesus, tired as he was from the journey, sat down by the well. It was about noon.

When a Samaritan woman came to draw water, Jesus said to her, "Will you give me a drink?" (His disciples had gone into the town to buy food.) The Samaritan woman said to him, "You are a Jew and I am a Samaritan woman. How can you ask me for a drink?" (For Jews do not associate with

Samaritans.)Jesus answered her,"If you knew the gift of God and who it is that asks you for a drink, you would have asked him and he would have given you living water.""Sir," the woman said,"you have nothing to draw with and the well is deep. Where can you get this living water? Are you greater than our father Jacob, who gave us the well and drank from it himself, as did also his sons and his livestock?"Jesus answered,"Everyone who drinks this water will be thirsty again, but whoever drinks the water I give them will never thirst. Indeed, the water I give them will become in them a spring of water welling up to eternal life." The woman said to him,"Sir, give me this water so that I won't get thirsty and have to keep coming here to draw water." He told her,"Go, call your husband and come back.""I have no husband," she replied. Jesus said to her,"You are right when you say you have no husband. The fact is, you have had five husbands, and the man you now have is not your husband. What you have just said is quite true." Sir, the woman said,"I can see that you are a prophet. Our fathers worshiped on this mountain, but you Jews claim that the place where we must worship is in Jerusalem." Jesus declared,"Believe me, a time is coming when you will worship the Father neither on this mountain nor in Jerusalem. You Samaritans worship what you do not know; we worship what we do know, for salvation is from the Jews. Yet a time is coming and has now come when the true worshipers will worship the Father in the Spirit and in truth, for they are the kind of worshipers the Father seeks. God is spirit, and his worshipers must worship in the Spirit and in truth." The woman said,"I know that Messiah" (called Christ)"is coming. When he comes, he will explain everything to us." Then Jesus declared,"I, the one speaking to you—I am he." Just then his disciples returned and were surprised to find him talking with a woman. But no one asked,"What do you want?" or"Why are you talking with her?" Then, leaving her water jar, the woman went back to the town and said to the people,"Come, see a man who told me everything I ever did. Could this be the Messiah?" (John 4:5–26)

Greetings: "Will you give me a drink?" (John4:7).

Water is used as a field material for a woman at a well in Sychar, Samaria. It is an onsite topic and uses onsite language. These are the first words Jesus spoke when he was thirsty.

Reaction: "You are a Jew, and I am a Samaritan woman. How can you ask me for a drink?" (John 4:9).

The woman reacts negatively. It shows the relationship between the Jews and the Samaritans. A long time ago, when Nehemiah's temple was reconstructed, the Samaritans, who were of mixed race, did not participate in rebuilding the temple, which worsened the hostile relationship. However, we can see an economic relationship at the time, not a complete disconnection, as the disciples went to get food at the village of Sychar.

Marshal: "If you knew the gift of God and who it is that asks you for a drink, you would have asked him and he would have given you living water" (John 4:10).

Jesus used marshal. Its affect arouses curiosity and focuses the listener's thinking to, *Who is he? What is spring water?* These veiled words aroused a woman's curiosity and led her to think. The subjunctive used is a very natural and useful way of expressing one's intentions indirectly in response to a question asked by a woman who is bewildered. It is a useful tool to overcome the awkward situation of being speechless in a conversation, which could lead to taking an offensive stance.

We can also see the use of counterparty-centric conversations. How insightful and precise are his words to the needs of this Samaritan woman. Jesus already knew her need and would provide it.

Reaction: "Sir, you have nothing to draw with, and the well is deep. Where can you get this living water? Are you greater than our father Jacob, who gave us the well and drank from it himself, as did also his sons and his livestock?" (John 4:12).

It means that you say that you are the giver of the gift of God, but how can you give me living water? Isn't it impossible? Despite the denial, the woman's curiosity continues. She asks a rhetorical question, expecting a negative answer. This part is also the same as the question in the conversation with the Jews:"What sign then will you give that we may see it and believe you? What will you do?" (John 6:30).

Supplementary Explanation: "Everyone who drinks this water will be thirsty again, but whoever drinks the water I give them will never thirst. Indeed, the water I give them will become in them a spring of water welling up to eternal life" (John 4: 13–14).

This woman now understands that living water is taken from the bottom of the well, not from the top. Just as Nicodemus fell into a contradiction in interpreting being born again as flesh, this woman tries to understand spiritual things only as physical ones.

Reaction: "Sir, give me this water so that I won't get thirsty and have to keep coming here to draw water" (John 4:15).

As a spiritually dull woman, this is a natural reaction. This her conversation didn't go any further. It then draws parallels.

Rebuke: "Go, call your husband and come back" (John 4:16).

At this point, a reprimand is given. In counter-centered conversations, the straightforward demands of, "go and call your husband," urge her to look at herself. This is also seen in the rebuke of Nicodemus in an earlier conversation: "You are Israel's teacher, and do you not understand these things?" (John 3:10). Here, rebuke is used to awaken spiritual ignorance, and it sounds no longer strange as the intimacy has changed the perspective of Jesus from Jew to a teacher. Opponent-centered conversations go straight inward, and this question makes her look inside herself.

Reaction: "I have no husband" (John 4:17).

The woman's conversation appears to be completely different from the noncooperative attitude she first displayed. She thinks of her current husband and soon looks back on her shameful life. The talkative woman answers briefly and concisely, and then remains silent. It hints at the hardship and suffering of her present self. The sixth man she now lives with cannot be her husband. She must have felt that Jesus's asking did not mean simply about her husband but more. It must have sounded closer to a demand for her to reveal what was hidden inside her.

Rebuke: "You are right when you say you have no husband. The fact is, you have had five husbands, and the man you now have is not your husband. What you have just said is quite true" (John 4:17–18).

Jesus's point of view made her truly look at herself. This woman's eyes are finally opened through the rebuke. Jesus has known this woman from the beginning, and he already got the answer. During conversations she began to realize that it was not just the water she was thinking of.

Reaction: "Sir, I can see that you are a prophet. Our fathers worshiped on this mountain, but you Jews claim that the place where we must worship is in Jerusalem" (John 4:20).

This woman's eyes adjusted and she now saw a prophet. As Jesus's title changed from sir to that of a prophet, her spiritual eyes gradually opened. The woman's heart was drawn to this prophet, and she longed for salvation from her unhappy and immoral reality. Avoiding the awkward situation by breaking the silence, the woman asked about the place of worship. It indicated her last stronghold was hope in God. "How can I meet God?" she asked, which led to the questions, "Where should I worship?""So can I offer it from the mountain Scheme on the scope of mountain Grishim?"

She was now looking for a way to salvation, and her soul's redemption her deepest aspiration. This thirst for God and eternal life were deeper than anything else. Earlier, even Nicodemus, who seemed to have everything, had the same thirst. It was the driving force that made him go to visit late at night, even at the cost of his pride.

Application: "Believe me, a time is coming when you will worship the Father neither on this mountain nor in Jerusalem. You Samaritans worship what you do not know; we worship what we do know, for salvation is from the Jews. Yet a time is coming and has now come when the true worshipers will worship the Father in the Spirit and in truth, for they are the kind of worshipers the Father seeks. God is spirit, and his worshipers must worship in the Spirit and in truth" (John 4:21–24).

The Word of truth applied that meets her expectations and needs.

Reaction: "I know that Messiah (called Christ) is coming. When he comes, he will explain everything to us" (John 4:25).

The ongoing conversation gradually shifted this woman's perspective of Jesus from a Jew to a prophet and a Messiah. He would not be qualified to proclaim this marvelous plan if not the Messiah. Her eyes were coming to terms with the possibility that he might be the Messiah. In the case of this Samaritan woman, the Lord knew her and led her to self-awareness. He took care of the woman's soul and led her to a confession of her own, even though it took some time.

This woman's eyes were drawn from the prophet to the possibility of the Messiah. The moment arrived, and the positive answer met her requirements.

Invitation: "I, the one speaking to you—I am he" (John 4:26).

Jesus encouraged the Samaritan woman and proclaimed a God who sought worship in spirit and truth. The power of marshal is that it brings one back to the spiritual perspective, and at some point, everything suddenly becomes apparent. This woman now fully understood what the marshal meant: "I asked you for a little water. But you are hesitating. Had you known that I am the Messiah, you would have asked for a gift from heaven. Then, without hesitation, I would have immediately given you living water without ever thirsting."She must have realized the meaning of the first marshal. Like Nicodemus, who found the appearance of the Messiah in the case of the brass serpent, this woman's thirsty spirit also met the Messiah, and her doubts soon disappeared.

Her deep spiritual longing led her to find the Messiah, who had also found her and, most astonishingly, was now speaking to her. The gift of a thirsty spring water gushed to her, offering everlasting life. This woman's actions revealed her confession: She left water jars behind and went into the town and called out to the people, "Come, see a man who told me everything I ever did. Could this be the Christ?" (John 4:29).A soul that was forever longing met a new and amazing world instantly.[17]

2. CONVERSATION WITH THE JEWS THE DAY AFTER MIRACLE OF FIVE LOAVES AND TWO FISHES

Once the crowd realized that neither Jesus nor his disciples were there, they got into the boats and went to Capernaum in search of Jesus. When they found him on the other side of the lake, they asked him,"Rabbi, when did you get here?" Jesus answered,"Very truly I tell you, you are looking for me, not because you saw miraculous signs I

---

[17] William Hendriksen, *Gospel of John* (1959) See chapter 4, pp. 153–169.

performed but because you ate the loaves and had your fill. Do not work for food that spoils, but for food that endures to eternal life, which the Son of Man will give you. For on him God the Father has placed his seal of approval." Then they asked him, "What must we do to do the works God requires?" Jesus answered, "The work of God is this: to believe in the one he has sent." So they asked him, "What sign then will you give that we may see it and believe you? What will you do? Our forefathers ate the manna in the desert; as it is written: 'He gave them bread from heaven to eat.'" Jesus said to them, "Very truly I tell you, it is not Moses who has given you the bread from heaven, but it is my Father who gives you the true bread from heaven. For the bread of God is he who comes down from heaven and gives life to the world.""Sir," they said, "always give us this bread." Then Jesus declared, "I am the bread of life. Whoever comes to me will never go hungry, and he who believes in me will never be thirsty. But as I told you, you have seen me and still you do not believe. All those the Father gives me will come to me, and whoever comes to me I will never drive away. For I have come down from heaven not to do my will but to do the will of him who sent me. And this is the will of him who sent me, that I shall lose none of all those he has given me, but raise them up at the last day. For my Father's will is that everyone who looks to the Son and believes in him shall have eternal life, and I will raise him up at the last day." At this the Jews began to grumble about him because he said, "I am the bread that came down from heaven." They said,"Is this not Jesus, the Son of Joseph, whose father and mother we know? How can he now say, 'I came down from heaven'?""Stop grumbling among yourselves," Jesus answered."No one can come to me unless the Father who sent me draws them, and I will raise them up at the last day. It is written in the Prophets: 'They will all be taught by God.' Everyone who has heard the Father and learns from him comes to me.

No one has seen the Father except the one who is from God; only he has seen the Father. Very truly I tell you, the one who believes has eternal life. I am the bread of life. Your ancestors ate the manna in the wilderness, yet they died. But here is the bread that comes down from heaven, which anyone may eat and not die. I am the living bread that came down from heaven. Whoever eats of this bread will live forever. This bread is my flesh, which I will give for the life of the world." Then the Jews began to argue sharply among themselves,"How can this man give us his flesh to eat?" Jesus said to them,"Very truly I tell you, unless you eat the flesh of the Son of Man and drink his blood, you have no life in you. Whoever eats my flesh and drinks my blood has eternal life, and I will raise him up at the last day. For my flesh is real food and my blood is real drink. Whoever eats my flesh and drinks my blood remains in me, and I in them. Just as the living Father sent me and I live because of the Father, so the one who feeds on me will live because of me. This is the bread that came down from heaven. Your ancestors ate manna and died, but whoever feeds on this bread will live forever."

He said this while teaching in the synagogue in Capernaum.

On hearing it, many of his disciples said,"This is a hard teaching. Who can accept it?" Aware that his disciples were grumbling about this, Jesus said to them,"Does this offend you? Then what if you see the Son of Man ascend to where he was before! The Spirit gives life; the flesh counts for nothing. The words I have spoken to you—they are full of the Spirit and life. Yet there are some of you who do not believe." For Jesus had known from the beginning which of them did not believe and who would betray him. He went on to say,"This is why I told you that no one can come to me unless the Father has enabled them." From this time, many of his disciples turned back and no longer followed him. "You do not want to leave too, do you?" Jesus asked the Twelve. Simon Peter answered him,"Lord, to whom we shall go? You have the words of eternal life. We have come to believe and to know that you are the Holy One of God." (John 6:24–69)

Greetings: "Rabbi, when did you get here?" (John 6:25).
After the great miracle—feeding more than five thousand men with five small barley loaves and two small fishes—the crowd saw that there was only one boat that Jesus was on. After the disciples left the boat, some walked along the coastline, and some crossed the lake by the merchant carrier ships that gathered from around Tiberius.

It seems that it was between three and six in the morning when Jesus reached Gennesaret. Then, after reaching Capernaum sometime later that morning, the crowd came through the port, found Jesus, and asked, "Rabbi, when did you get here?" They said on the extended line of yesterday. Their fierce demand to make Jesus the King from yesterday never changed.

Marshal:"Very truly I tell you, you are looking for me, not because you saw signs I performed but because you ate the loaves and had your fill. Do not work for food that spoils, but for food that endures to eternal life, which the Son of Man will give you. For on him, God the Father has placed his seal of approval" (John 6:27).

Marshal was given. Audiences were left to wonder the meaning of "working for food that lasts forever and who is the Son of Man that gives it?"It made them think deeply. This expression was used differently by the Samaritan woman, concealing the Son of Man and revealing it later. It is the same pattern; the "he" identity is hidden and then revealed. If you knew the gift of God and who it is that asks you for a drink, you would have asked him, and he would have given you living water.

Response: What must we do to do the works God requires?

It was their first response. The crowd did not immediately understand the spiritual marshal. Like the Samaritan woman, who also interpreted the Spiritual as physical, they wanted to make Jesus the King and enter Jerusalem with him as their revolutionary leader.

Their reply referred to the administrative tasks to be performed after the fall of Rome and the conquest of Jerusalem. They had in mind the tasks required of various positions, such as administrative or defensive roles. Like Nicodemus, they also thought that human devotion and effort are examples of God's work.

Supplementary Explanation: The work of God is this: to believe in the one he has sent. Salvation is not based on human devotion and effort, as in the case of Nicodemus. It is realized through a new perspective of "belief in the one sent by God."

Reaction: "What sign then will you give that we may see it and believe you? What will you do? Our forefathers ate the manna in the desert; as written: 'He gave them bread from heaven to eat'" (John 6:30–31).

Their curiosity led directly to the next question: "You say that you are the one sent by God, can you show us a sign?"Despite the denial, the curiosity continued. "What are the signs you are doing to make us believe?"And, "what are you doing?" Both rhetorical questions expected a negative answer.

They mentioned that their ancestors ate the manna in the wilderness. And Moses gave them bread from heaven to eat. To put it simply, "Are you greater than Moses, who gave our forefathers the manna?"The Samaritan woman had also asked, "Are you greater than our father Jacob?" (John 4:12).Like Nicodemus and the Samaritan woman, the crowd had no idea that their conversation was leading in the direction Jesus intended.

Supplementary Explanation:"Very truly I tell you, it is not Moses who has given you the bread from heaven but it is my Father who gives you the true bread from heaven. For the bread from God is he who comes down from heaven and gives life to the world" (John 6:32–34).

Comparisons of the bread of Moses and the true bread of heaven are supplemented and explained very naturally in line with people's thoughts and questions.

This part also uses the same pattern as when Jesus said to the Samaritan woman, "everyone who drinks this water will be thirsty again, but whoever drinks the water I give them will never thirst. Indeed, the water I give them will become in them a spring of water welling up to eternal life" (John 4:13–14).

Reaction: "Sir, always give us this bread" (John 6:34).

This part is also the same as the Samaritan woman's order:

"Sir, give me this water so that I won't get thirsty and have to keep coming here to draw water" (John 4:15)

Rebuke: "But as I told you, you have seen me and still you do not believe. All those the Father gives me will come to me, and whoever comes to me I will never drive away. For I have come down from heaven not to do my will but to do the will of him who sent me. And this is the will of him who sent me, that I shall lose none of all those he has given me, but raise them up at the last day. For my Father's will is that everyone who looks to the Son and believes in him shall have eternal life, and I will raise them up at the last day" (John 6:36–40).

A call for reproof is given to those spiritually unaware and wandering. The hidden "Son of Man" is revealed to be Jesus himself—the same as he revealed himself to the Samaritan woman.

Those who come from the Father are given the responsibility to come to the Son, and Jesus warmly welcomes all who come to him. Those who belong to the Son are not rejected by God but are welcomed and accepted without exception because the Father and the Son are one. The bread of eternal life is the Word of Jesus Christ, and is received through faith, just like eating bread.

But no one can come to Jesus unless the Father draws. It is also said that unless one belongs to the Father, he cannot see and believe in Jesus as the Son of Man. Just as the Holy Spirit was explained to Nicodemus through the wind, its randomness is also emphasized here. Just as the wind blows freely and unhindered, salvation is only attained by God's arbitrary grace and his work.

Reaction: "Is this not Jesus, the Son of Joseph, whose father and mother we know? How can he now say, 'I came down from heaven'" (John 6:42).

Their reaction was very negative. The Jews only looked at Jesus in the flesh and disregarded his spiritual vision. They rejected the Son of God and strove to reduce the spiritual Messiah to a flesh one. They reacted with contempt, denying him because, like everyone else, he was born with a body.

Application: "Very truly I tell you; the one who believes has eternal life. I am the bread of life. Your ancestors ate the manna in the wilderness, yet they died. But here is the bread that comes down from heaven, which a man may eat and not die. I am the living bread that came down from heaven. whoever eats this bread will live forever. This bread is my flesh, which I will give for the life of the world. I am the living bread that came down from heaven; if anyone eats this bread, he will live forever. The bread that I will give is my flesh for the life of the world" (John 6:47–51).

God's sovereign guidance and the living bread that comes from heaven are compared with the manna in the wilderness.

Reaction: "How can this man give us his flesh to eat?" (John 6:52).

They began to argue sharply among themselves. Their reactions turned into resistance rather than negativity. The people in the crowd struggled with each other and became more stubborn. This response was completely different from Nicodemus's polite questioning or the Samaritan woman's supplication.

Invitation: "Very truly I tell you, unless you eat the flesh of the Son of Man and drink his blood, you have no life in you. Whoever eats my flesh and drinks my blood has eternal life, and I will raise him up at the last day. For my flesh is real food and my blood is real drink. Whoever eats my flesh and drinks my blood remains in me, and I in them. Just as the living Father sent me and I live because of the Father, so the one who feeds on me will live because of me. This is the bread that came down from heaven. Your ancestors ate manna and died, but whoever feeds on this bread will live forever" (John 6:53–58).

It was the word of eternal life to those who believed, but to the unbeliever, it sounded like both a rebuke and a warning. It is one's own choice and responsibility. Just as Jesus gave the invitation to eternal life at the end of the conversations, it is given to them, "whoever eats my flesh and drinks my blood has eternal life, and I will raise him up at the last day."

Offers were put to Nicodemus politely:"whoever lives by the truth comes into the light, so that it may be seen plainly that what they have done has been done in the sight of God" (John 3:21), and to the Samaritan woman warmly: "I, the one speaking to you—I am he (The Messiah you are looking for)" (John 4:26). Here, Jesus gave an invitation to a Jew in spite of their sharp argument and denial under a resistance atmosphere.

Flesh and blood is a spiritual expression made with the sacrifice of the cross in mind. The Jews understood that eating flesh and drinking blood meant cannibalism. Not listening to marshal spiritually will make one fall into a deeper pit. Many of his disciples turned their backs on Jesus and no longer followed him.

After hearing the words, the audience showed three reactions. The hostile religious leaders—unbelieving, self-satisfying, reverence for tradition—and their followers who reject Jesus's words without any attempt at spiritual understanding remained unchanged. They gossiped and even quarreled with each other. Those among them from Galilee relegated Jesus to being only the son of Joseph and left him.

Many who followed Jesus regularly found his request too unrealistic and unacceptable. It was not that the sermons were difficult to understand, but rather, it was due to the hardness of their hearts. They were happy to cling to their practical needs rather than commit to his sermons on eternal life. It was not because they are walking in the truth of Jesus Christ but because they differed from their ultimate goals of being full and satisfied. Jesus pointed out that one must eat the true bread from heaven to live, not the manna for the flesh, which they had heard so much about. They did not want to accept that they had to eat his flesh and drink his blood. Torn my body and giving my blood refers to my spirit, my whole person. People who ate manna for the flesh died even after eating it, but only the true bread that gives life leads to eternal life.

The life of a new disciple in Christ was presented and invited, but they rejected, concerned only with the present physical blessings. The life of a disciple was not what they wanted.

When most of the crowd saw the amazing miracle of feeding more than the five thousand men with five barley loaves and two fishes, they ate the miraculous food. But they paid little or no attention to the events taking place. Instead, they focused on the bread that would fill them. Although Jesus manifested his miraculous power, it was not used as a direct tool to bring about change in people. Rather, Jesus rebuked the generation that demanded miracles for their lack of faith: "A wicked and adulterous generation asks for a miraculous sign! But none will be given it except the sign of the prophet Jonah" (Matthew 12:39).

Thrill seekers! They believe in miracles but do not believe in God.[18] It's not that the miracles are few; it's the lack of faith. It is why Jesus told us that no one could come to him unless the Father had enabled the person.

But the twelve disciples went forth with a more confident confession. Jesus' words, "You do not want to leave too, do you?" (John 6:67) were given to elicit a positive confession.

Peter's confession of outstanding spirituality follows: "Lord, to whom we shall go? You have the words of eternal life. We have come to believe and to know that you are the Holy One of God" (John 6:68–69).

Their eyes today have changed from yesterday's view. They are the true disciples who have realized the truth of Jesus, forsaken everything, and chosen to follow him.

It is the confession of those who know, accept, acknowledge, and unite with the truth that the true bread is the Word of Jesus, and that bread is the Spirit and life.

---

[18] William Hendriksen, *Gospel of John* (1959) See chapter 6, p. 241.

In this dialogue, we can see that supplementary explanations are repeatedly given, and the intensity of the rebuke is measured according to their levels of response. The application was given to the audience in the form of, "Very truly I say to you ..."

It is notable that Jesus expressed faith by eating his flesh and drinking his blood. The answer to the question, "What is it like to believe in Jesus?" was surprisingly explained in the argument with the Jews using bread, which was the material onsite. "Whoever eats my flesh and drinks my blood remains in me, and I in him. Just as the living Father sent me and I live because of the Father, so the one who feeds on me will live because of me" (John 6:56–57).

It's amazing how Jesus explains what it means to believe in him and what it means to have eternal life in such a concise way. His flesh is the true food, and his blood is the true drink—a spiritual expression that those who eat and drink it will have eternal life (John 6:41–58). It explains the relationship between, "eating my flesh and my blood."Just as the body is nourished, eating Jesus's flesh and drinking his blood to have eternal life are also necessary.

Who must eat Christ, the bread of life, have a life. It means accepting Jesus, acknowledging him, and uniting with him, just as Jesus lives because of the Father. And as bread and drink were offered and accepted, Christ's sacrifice is offered to and accepted by believers. Man needs to eat bread to live, just as food and drinks must be eaten rather than tasted. Blood and flesh are digested in the body to make up one's body, and they become inseparable and the power that sustains oneself. The definition of faith taught by Jesus was not simply to receive Jesus as the Savior intellectually but to live by the blood and flesh of Jesus.[19]

---

[19] William Hendriksen, *Gospel of John* (1959) See chapter 6, pp. 242–244.

Even as he spoke, many put their faith in him. To the Jews who had believed him, Jesus said, "If you hold to my teaching, you are really my disciples. Then you will know the truth, and the truth will set you free." They answered him, "We are Abraham's descendants and have never been slaves of anyone. How can you say that we shall be set free?" Jesus replied, "Very truly I tell you, everyone who sins is a slave to sin. Now a slave has no permanent place in the family, but a son belongs to it forever. So if the Son sets you free, you will be free indeed. I know that you are Abraham's descendants. Yet you are ready to kill me, because you have no room for my word. I am telling you what I have seen in the Father's presence, and you do what you have heard from your father.""Abraham is our father," they answered. "If you were Abraham's children," said Jesus, "then you would do what Abraham did. As it is, you are looking for a way to kill me, a man who has told you the truth that I heard from God. Abraham did not do such things. You are doing the works of your own father.""We are not illegitimate children," they protested. "The only Father we have is God himself." Jesus said to them, "If God were your Father, you would love me, for I came from God. I have not come on my own; God sent me. Why is my language not clear to you? Because you are unable to hear what I say. You belong to your Father, the devil, and you want to carry out your father's desire. He was a murderer from the beginning, not holding to the truth, for there is no truth in him. When he lies, he speaks his native language, for he is a liar and the father of lies. Yet because I tell the truth, you do not believe me! Can any of you prove me guilty of sin? If I am telling the truth, why don't you believe me? whoever belongs to God hears what God says. The reason you do not hear is that you do not belong to God." The Jews answered him, "Aren't we right in saying that you are a Samaritan and demon-possessed?""I am not possessed by a demon," said Jesus, "but I honor my Father and you dishonor me. I am not seeking glory for myself; but there is one who seeks it, and he is the judge. Very truly I tell you whoever obeys my word will never see death." At this the Jews exclaimed, "Now we know that you are demon-possessed! Abraham died and so did the prophets, yet you say that whoever obeys your word will never taste death. Are you greater than our father Abraham? He died, and so did the prophets. Who do you think you are?" Jesus replied, "If I glorify myself, my glory means nothing. My Father, whom you claim as your God, is the one who glorifies me. Though you do not know him, I know him. If I said I did not, I would be a liar like you, but I do know him and obey his word. Your father Abraham rejoiced at the thought of seeing my day; he saw it and was glad." You are not yet fifty years old,"they said to him, "and you have seen Abraham!""Very truly I tell you," Jesus answered, "before Abraham was born, I am!" At this, they picked up stones to stone him, but

Jesus hid himself, slipping away from the temple grounds. (John 8:30–59)

We can also see Jesus's four-step dialogue evangelism amid conflict. It can be briefly summarized as follows.

Marshal: "If you hold to my teaching, you are really my disciples. Then you will know the truth, and the truth will set you free" (John 8:31–32).

Reaction: "We are Abraham's descendants and have never been slaves of anyone. How can you say that we shall be set free?" (John 8:33).

Even if the transmission of words comes out of my mouth, the ears hear differently depending on the listeners' hearts. To them, the word "freedom" is heard as being a "servant".

Supplementary Expression: "Very truly I tell you, everyone who sins is a slave to sin. A slave has no permanent place in the family, but a son belongs to it forever. So if the Son sets you free, you will be free indeed" (John 8:34–36).

Reaction: "Abraham is our father" (John 8:39).

They expressed their religious and spiritual orthodoxy. The word "servant" was not appropriate for those who prided themselves on not being slaves, even though they were a colony of Rome. They protested that they were not illegitimate children: "The only Father we have is God himself."

It is an indirect expression of denying the virgin birth and saying that Jesus is a Samaritan, an illegitimate child of Jesus.

Rebuke: "As it is, you are looking for a way to kill me, a man who has told you the truth I heard from God" (John 8:40).

These words became the trigger for the conflict to heat up. Jesus intentionally exposed their lies and hypocrisies full of murderous intent.

Rebukes for persuasion are given several times: "Why is my language not clear to you? Because you are unable to hear what I say" (John 8:43); "Yet because I tell the truth, you do not believe me!" (John 8:45); "The reason you do not hear is that you do not belong to God" (John 8:47); and, "but I honor my Father, and you dishonor me" (John 8:49).

Reaction: "Aren't we right in saying that you are a Samaritan and demon-possessed?" (John 8:48).

The first filtered expression, "We are not illegitimate children"(John 8:41),was turned blatantly and assertively that, "You are Samaritans." Not only that, but they also added a comment that said, "will never die," and denounced, "Now we know that you are demon-possessed!"Their attitude toward the truth of Jesus's claims not only shows no change but accelerates toward active resistance.

Application: "Very truly I tell you, whoever obey my word will never see death" (John 8:51).

Reaction: "Are you greater than our father, Abraham? He died, and so did the prophets. Who do you think you are?" (John 8:52).

The same question was asked as in the cases of Nicodemus or and the Samaritan woman.

Supplementary Expression:"Your father Abraham rejoiced at the thought of seeing my day; he saw it and was glad" (John 8:56).

Reaction: "You are not yet fifty years old, and you have seen Abraham!" (John 8:57).

Invitation:"I tell you the truth before Abraham was born, I am!" (John 8:58).This statement contains an invitation.

Reaction: "They picked up stones to stone him" (John 8:59).

They were about to pick up stones to stone him, but Jesus hid and slipped away from the temple grounds.

Contents and effective expression used here can be summarized as follows.

Marshal was given: "If you hold to my teaching, you are really my disciples. Then you will know the truth, and the truth will set you free" (John 8–31).

Supplementary explanations were given according to the response. A call for reproof were given appropriately and weighted according to the degree of response: "As it is, you are looking for a way to kill me, a man who has told you the truth that I heard from God" (John 8:40); "Why is my language not clear to you? Because you are unable to hear what I say" (John 8:43); "Yet because I tell the truth you do not believe me!" (John 8:45); and, "but I honor my Father and you dishonor me" (John 8:49).

As a manner of a strong application and invitation to the audience, Jesus here used it in the form, "Very truly I say to you." This expression seems to approach very impressively to the audience, likely, "Very truly I tell you, the one who believe has eternal life"(John 6:47).

If Nicodemus was politely invited, the Jews were now being invited with severe reproach: "He who belongs to God hears what God says. The reason you do not hear is that you do not belong to God" (John8:47), and, "You belong to your father, the devil, and you want to carry out your father's desire. He was a murderer from the beginning, not holding to the truth, for there is no truth in him. He speaks his native language when he lies, for he is a liar and the father of lies" (John8:44).

Logic development was led by the counterpart-centered dialogue method, and clear differences in positions were well expressed through contrasting expressions. In contrast to expressions such as, "for I did not speak of my own accord, but the Father who sent me commanded me what to say and how to say it" (John12:49), or, "I am telling you what I have seen in the Father's presence, and you do what you have heard from your father" (John 8:38).

As a tool for persuasion, the proposition "father and son" is used as a metaphor, and the subjunctive is used: "you do not know him, I know him. If I said I did not, I would be a liar like you, but I do know him and keep his word" (John 8:55), and, "If God were your Father, you would love me, for I came from God and now am here. I have not come on my own, but he sent me" (John8:42).

About the Author

Author HeungSik, Lee was born in 1954 in Koje Island, South Korea, and grew up under the religious Christian tradition inherited from his grandmother. His mother, who has sincere belief, left him to the respected pastor (the late missionary Jong-cheol Lee, who belongs to the most conservative Presbyterian Church) There he spent his childhood.

He majored in international trade and worked in the shipping industries for a long time. He married Sarah and had two sons and a daughter.

He found many Christians fail to defend Christianity especially in their daily activities even though they had faith. He also has suffered from this problem, which had been left as a barren ground to everyone. It made him question of how to overcome this gap between faith and reality.

After immigrating to New Zealand in 2002, By chance, through the one of commentary books of "Gospel of John" he could find an answer to his long-standing anguish. He could meet Jesus closest and found that the style of conversation shown by Jesus will be the model that of our Christians should pursue today and is the most practical and useful path in reality. He stressed that if our daily encounters and conversation start with the flesh and ends with the flesh we might lose the most effective opportunity to save the spirit.

He wrote this book for readers who were asking how to defend the faith and how to say in daily encounters and conversations, together with the second generation of immigrants who are born abroad.

His biblical approach and spiritual insights provided readers with a clear picture of Christian life and spiritual refreshment.

He presently attends Hanouri Korean Presbyterian Church in NZ and now serves Retreat House for missionaries together with his wife Sarah and her sister's family.

Printed in the United States
by Baker & Taylor Publisher Services